George McLean Harper

The legend of the Holy Grail

George McLean Harper

The legend of the Holy Grail

ISBN/EAN: 9783742836755

Manufactured in Europe, USA, Canada, Australia, Japa

Cover: Foto ©Lupo / pixelio.de

Manufactured and distributed by brebook publishing software
(www.brebook.com)

George McLean Harper

The legend of the Holy Grail

THE

LEGEND OF THE HOLY GRAIL

DISSERTATION PRESENTED TO THE FACULTY OF
PRINCETON COLLEGE FOR THE DEGREE
OF DOCTOR OF PHILOSOPHY

BY

GEORGE McLEAN HARPER

ASSISTANT PROFESSOR OF FRENCH IN PRINCETON COLLEGE

———————

[Reprinted from the *Publications of the Modern Language Association of America*, New Series, Vol. I, No. 1]

———————

BALTIMORE
THE MODERN LANGUAGE ASSOCIATION OF AMERICA
1893

Of the main streams of medieval poetry three were so seriously checked by the Renascence that they are only at the present day beginning to flow again as literary influences. They are the Norse Edda, the German Heldensage, and the Celtic national cycle. From these abundant sources the literature of Europe during the sixteenth, seventeenth, and eighteenth centuries drew but little.

Spenser and Shakespeare, Racine and Molière, who all were sturdy robbers of old plots and incidents, we seldom find turning to the Middle Ages for material. Fashion and the times pointed to other springs, to the Greek and Latin, and then to the Hebrew classics. In the eighteenth century recourse was had to them still less than in the two preceding. When even Dante was unknown to most men and unappreciated by all, it could not be expected that people of "sensibility" should relish the barbaric utterances of our northern fathers. And indeed, considering how recent has been the work of editing and translating the manuscripts containing these three stupendous bodies of poetry, we cannot censure a Voltaire or a Dryden for neglecting them, but can only wonder what the accomplished versifiers of their times would have achieved with this material, so much more suggestive than any they employed. Probably nothing of note, for it has been reserved to our century to find itself in sympathy with the eleventh, twelfth, thirteenth, and early fourteenth. These centuries, the heart of the Middle Ages, were an epoch of unconscious self-development, an epoch of bold experimentation and independent working-out of native ideas. Shut off from the quarries of the past by an abyss of ignorance, the thinkers of that day built on such foundations as they could themselves construct. They possessed that lightness of fancy, that brilliant self-assertion, which are

3

among the marks of young creative genius in the full consciousness of its strength and liberty. Apart from their
deference to the precepts of Aristotle, whom only the most
learned even half understood, they were bound to no such
distinct traditions in philosophy, religion, political economy,
poetics, and all other lines of intellectual effort as were their
successors of the next age. They were not characterized by great
respect for authority, since authorities were few and obscurely
comprehended. They were not much given to dogmatic assertion. The centuries of creed-making and creed-imposing preceded and followed this central period of the Middle Ages, which
was an epoch rather of ready and fanciful invention, of keen
delight in artistic construction, of liberty to think. It is a mark
of wonderful vigor and elasticity that Western Christendom,
while still under the influence of Germanic and Celtic paganism,
could assimilate so much as it did of two such diverse and alien
matters as the learning of the Greeks and of the Arabs. And
this, during the Crusades, was quickly and gaily accomplished.
The grotesqueness of medieval art, so often patronizingly
alluded to by eighteenth-century writers and even by Goethe,
is but evidence of that exuberant and unreflecting vitality.

This abundance of life, this zest in expression, manifested
themselves in all sorts of wayward fashions, very distasteful to
the more methodical people of the Renascence. In religion
they gave birth to a multitude of bold inventions, to an extra-
ordinary development of legends and heresies and cathedrals
and pious orders. In philosophy the venturesome mysticism
of Eckart, Tauler, and Suso was tolerated side by side with the
orthodox system of Thomas Aquinas, anchored to authority at
every point; and both in turn left room for the still barer and
safer scholasticism of Raymond Lully, who taught how to solve
all the problems of logic and metaphysics by means of a card-
board machine. In literature—but here all was invention, and
seldom has poetry been so truly a liberal art. No bonds had
yet been laid on the creative instinct, and even theology, as we
have seen, had not yet entered the prison-house of either Roman

or Protestant dogmatism. Religious and poetical expression were still unsevered, as the feelings which prompt them frequently are; they are inseparable in Dante, in Saint Francis of Assisi, in Saint Catherine of Siena. It is in speaking of this period and of medieval literature that Renan eloquently exclaims: Qui osera dire où est ici-bas la limite de la raison et du songe? Lequel vaut mieux des instincts imaginatifs de l'homme ou d'une orthodoxie étroite qui prétend rester sensée en parlant des choses divines? Pour moi je préfère la franche mythologie, avec ses égarements, à une théologie si mesquine, si vulgaire, si incolore, que ce serait faire injure à Dieu de croire qu'après avoir fait le monde visible si beau, il eût fait le monde invisible si platement raisonnable.

The three streams of poetry which the diverting influence of classical models caused to dwindle for four hundred years and almost disappear have one common feature: they all arise in the remote fastnesses of heathen antiquity, they are all tinged with the dark waters of Druidical or Northern lore. The first of them, the Norse anthology—for the Edda songs can hardly be more than fragments of the body of mythology to which they bear witness—is of greater value than either of the others, both intrinsically and for purposes of historical science, comprising the earliest and most complete record we possess of the religious system of the primitive Teutonic race. But the day of renewed influence for the Edda is only just dawning, despite the labors of such popular interpreters as Karl Simrock and William Morris.

Celtic literature, however, has been hitherto the strongest of these influencing streams. Through filtration, when it was first put into writing, through translation, both medieval and modern, through an unperceived power of suggestion in all ages, it has affected European poetry from the Irish coast to the shores of the Euxine and from Norway to Spain. There has been forever in it a subtle sympathetic appeal to the finer poetic sense; not the sense which Homer satisfies with his clear, beautiful; vigorous action, nor that which the Song of Songs soothes with its languorous sweetness, but the nerve that vibrates to those delicate, fleeting touches which occasionally startle and hold us spell-bound in English poetry as nowhere else.   We hear this appeal in the unexpected change from the tempestuous workings of the first act of *Macbeth* to the soft breath of summer evening, when Duncan, unconscious of his doom, casting an untroubled eye up to the heavens, says to Banquo :

> "This castle hath a pleasant seat; the air
> Nimbly and sweetly recommends itself
> Unto our gentle senses."

and Banquo answers :

> "This guest of summer,
> The temple-haunting martlet, does approve,
> By his loved mansionry, that the heaven's breath
> Smells wooingly here: no jutty, frieze,
> Buttress, nor coign of vantage, but this bird
> Hath made his pendent bed and procreant cradle:
> Where they most breed and haunt, I have observed,
> The air is delicate."

We hear it again, but how changed, in Wordsworth's

> "Old, unhappy far-off things,
> And battles long ago."

And the same strain, just as melancholy, just as suggestive, just as haunting, with the same intimate apprehension of the workings of nature and the same plaintive yet distinct utterance, is audible in the ancient ballad of *The Twa Corbies*.   The one to the other says of the new slain knight, deserted by his false lady fair :

> "Ye'll sit on his white hause bane,
> And I'll pike out his bonny blue een:
> Wi' ae lock o' his gowden hair,
> We'll theek our nest when it grows bare."

The character of the Celts, proud and vindictive, shy and elusive, and strangely moved at times with a gay melancholy, is plainly discoverable in these passages.   Irish wit and Scottish music have this character, and I think the Highlander and the Breton exhibit it in their lives and speech. The feeling of interpenetration with external things, the passion for beauty which excludes all grossness, the despair of perfection which forbids the commonplace, the immanent persuasion of natural magic—these, then, are some of the marks of that Celtic spirit which with fairy lightness winged its unsubstantial way so fast into men's hearts, eight hundred years ago. No poetical influence was at that time half so widespread as that which started from Wales. In this fact there is a touching vindication of the Celtic race, a recompense to it, in the realm of mind, for its long-drawn material defeat.

The consciousness of this defeat can never have been more bitter than at the end of the eleventh century, when the Norman barons, with appetites whetted in Teutonic England, burst through the barriers of the Welsh mountains and all but completed the subjugation of that unhappy remnant whom Saxon and Dane had spared. The victory of their Saxon conquerors, six hundred years before, had been to the Celts at first like the going down of the world. It had seemed as if their own higher civilization, their new and enthusiastically entertained Christianity ought to save them. But nothing had availed. Accompanying this overthrow, and doubtless to console them for it, there was a revival of national poetry in the sixth century, of which many scattered traces have come down to us. Then succeeded an era which, according to the prevailing opinion, was one of rapid extinction. We frequently read of conquered races being exterminated, and it is generally stated that few if any Britons were left in England proper by the time of the Norman invasion; but there is a great deal of analogy, besides inherent improbability, against that conclusion and in favor of the opinion that there is still a considerable element of Celtic blood in the so-called Anglo-Saxon race, due to admixture before and during the eleventh century. But however that may be, there were free Celts in Wales at the

2

beginning of Norman rule, and in a little more than a hundred years they had lost their independence.

And now, at the beginning of the twelfth century, how stood the Celtic world? Whether in Brittany, Cornwall, Wales, Ireland, Scotland, or the Western Isles, they were a crushed, divided, and one would suppose humiliated race. But though politically almost annihilated, they were by no means humble. They had two titles, they thought, to glory. They remembered that they were the original possessors of the land. Their sense of antiquity was strengthened by a revival, in noble song, of the old heathen mythology, just as it had been revived in the days of Taliesin, after the Saxon conquest. Secondly, they were conscious of being older as a Christian people than either Saxons or Normans. They claimed an authority independent of Rome, or at least the original Irish church had done so, centuries before, and we may be sure the contention was remembered now. The Irish church in days gone by had kept alive the purest form of Christianity, and maintained the highest scholarship in Europe. It had been the great missionary and educational fountain. The tendency of the Celts in Great Britain and Ireland has at all times been towards separation from the type of worship and church government prevailing in England.

It was after a century of misfortune, when only their faith in their destiny and their consciousness of their distinction remained, that the Celtic spirit asserted itself. Then was manifested the power of a national ideal. To find courage for the losing struggle in which they were engaged, and especially to console themselves in the day of final disaster, they turned again to the songs of their fathers. As a result, not only had the Welsh themselves begun to see new meanings in their old poetry, but the stories of their heroes were brought to the attention of the outside world. Somewhere between 1135 and 1150 Geoffrey of Monmouth wrote his *Historia Britonum,* a legendary account of the supposed early kings of Britain, containing the prophecies of Merlin, the record of " the princes whose reign had preceded the birth of Jesus Christ, and of

Arthur and the princes who had reigned in Britain since the incarnation." Geoffrey declared that his book was an exact translation of a book in Celtic which Walter, archdeacon of Oxford, had brought into England from Brittany. The French critic Paulin Paris maintains that the original was more probably the Chronicle of Nennius, a Latin work of the ninth century; but in either case it was the main source of what English writers of the twelfth century, such as Henry of Huntingdon and William of Malmsbury, knew concerning the legendary history of the Celts. The *Historia Britonum* speedily attained a world-wide circulation, and meanwhile the task of arousing Celtic resistance went steadily on in Wales.

The reigns of the two Llewellyns, extending from 1195 to 1283, were marked by such an outburst of patriotic song as can be paralleled only by the Hebrew poetry of the exile. National heroes were brought to life again and warlike achievements of the great dead kings were invented with a boldness justified by the cause,—and by the result, for this fervor was not ineffectual; the invaders discovered an unexpected resistance and were held at bay until the policy and military prowess of Edward the First of England compelled an honorable submission. In their zeal to inspire courage by means of heroic memories from a distant past, the bards of the thirteenth century revived what was left in the Welsh mind of Druidical superstition. They often gave to their own exciting compositions the authority of poets belonging to the older generation, pretending to have found ancient books or to have received occult traditions. "Mysterious prophecies," says J. R. Green, "floated from lip to lip, till the name of Merlin was heard along the Seine and the Rhine. Medrawd and Arthur would appear once more on earth to fight over again the fatal battle of Camlan. The last conqueror of the Celtic race, Cadwallon, still lived to combat for his people. The supposed verses of Taliesin expressed the undying hope of a restoration of the Cymry." Augustin Thierry remarks (*Histoire de la Conquête de l'Angleterre*): "The reputation of the Welsh for prophecy in the Middle Ages came from their stubbornness in affirming the future of their race."

It will never be known how much of this poetry was really ancient and how much pure forgery. It may be doubted whether in those exciting times the bards themselves knew. All France and England became acquainted with the Welsh and Breton legends and predictions, largely through Geoffrey of Monmouth's work, which he revised and augmented from time to time, and of which manuscripts were numerous. The *Historia Britonum*, whether based on a Breton or a Latin book, derived its material ultimately from Armorican lays and legends. The encounter of Breton and Welsh stories and the harmony discovered between them concerning events supposed to have happened on British soil doubtless confirmed Geoffrey and others in a belief that their substance was historically true, and gave an impulse to further composition. The story of Arthur and his Round Table was accepted with especial readiness. "Charlemagne and Alexander, the sagas of Teutonic tribes, the tale of Imperial Rome itself, though still affording subject matter to the wandering jongleur or monkish annalist, paled before the fame of the British King. The instinct which led the twelfth and thirteenth centuries thus to place the Arthurian story above all others was a true one. It was charged with the spirit of romance, and they were pre-eminently the ages of the romantic temper."[1]

With characteristic levity the Welsh genius had failed to localize the legends. There was nothing in them to disturb the conquerors, who were charmed, rather, by their tender melancholy. "It is by this trait of idealism and universality," says M. Renan, "that the story of Arthur won such astonishing vogue throughout the whole world." So from this inward cause, no doubt, but also from the fact that Brittany too was Celtic and both Brittany and Wales were contiguous to great nations where French was the language of at least the upper

[1] Nutt: *The Legend of the Holy Grail*, p. 229.

classes, the body of Celtic legend was broken up and carried all over Western Europe with amazing rapidity. Thus from about 1145, when Geoffrey of Monmouth first opened the door, it was not a generation until this legendary matter was incorporated in all the romantic poetry of Christendom, and by the end of the century the assimilation was complete. The quickness and thoroughness of this absorption will be apparent later, when I shall present a list of the versions still extant of one story for which a Celtic origin is claimed.

It is only within the last sixty years that the vast body of romance which goes under the name of the Legend of the Holy Grail has been made the subject either of critical analysis or of literary reconstruction. Its earliest students suffered for lack of complete texts. Not all of the manuscripts up to that time discovered were yet available. Many of the conclusions reached, while testifying to great acumen, have been one after another proved inconsistent with new-found facts, and thus one of the most fascinating of poetical subjects has, from its difficulty, become scarcely less alluring as a field of scholarship. Several recent publications in particular have rendered untenable the views of many authorities still referred to, and have opened long reaches of speculation yet untrodden.

The latest stage of discussion began with the appearance of Birch-Hirschfeld's *Die Sage vom Gral*, in 1877 ; and the most recent contributions to it include, besides articles in specialist periodicals, the searching and all-embracing work of Alfred Nutt in the publications of the Folk-lore Society of England,[1] and the studies of the Oxford professor of Celtic.[2]

The appearance of so much new and valuable information reversing previous conceptions of the legend, justifies an attempt

---

[1] "Mabinogion Studies," by Alfred Nutt, in vol. V of *The Folk-lore Record*, London, 1882. "The Aryan Expulsion and Return Formula Among the Celts," in vol. IV of *The Folk-lore Record*, London ; "Studies on the Legend of the Holy Grail," in the publications of the Folk-lore Society, London, 1888.

[2] *Studies in the Arthurian Legend*, by John Rhŷs, M. A., Fellow of Jesus College and Professor of Celtic in the University of Oxford. Published at the Clarendon Press, 1891.

to present synthetically the history of its origin, spread, and influence. The accounts given in many popular works are seriously misleading. For instance, the article in the *Encyclopaedia Britannica*, ninth edition, by Thomas Arnold, presents an outline which was based largely on the edition of 1876 of Paulin Paris' *Les Romans de la Table Ronde*, and is in accordance with the view commonly entertained by all except the most recent students of the subject. It represents well enough the results of investigation prior to the last fifteen years. According to it "The 'Saint Greal' was the name given—if not originally, yet very soon after the conception was started—to the dish, or shallow bowl (in French *escuelle*) from which Jesus Christ was said to have eaten the paschal lamb on the evening of the Last Supper with his disciples. In the French prose romance of the *Saint Graal*, it is said that Joseph of Arimathea, having obtained leave from Pilate to take down the body of Jesus from the cross, proceeded first to the upper room where the supper was held and found there this vessel; then as he took down the Lord's dead body, he received into the vessel many drops of blood which issued from the still open wounds in his feet, hands, and side. . . . According to Catholic theology, where the body or the blood of Christ is, there, by virtue of the hypostatic union, are His soul and His divinity." It is then shown that the legend declares this holy vessel to have been brought to England and treasured there by the descendants of Joseph of Arimathea, who established the royal line of Britain. The presence of the vessel in the British Church sanctioned the latter's existence and gave virtue to its eucharist. The writer condenses Paulin Paris' theory of the origin of the legend as follows: "The original conception came from some Welsh monk or hermit who lived early in the eighth century; its guiding and essential import was an assertion for the British Church of an independent derivation of its Christianity direct from Palestine, and not through Rome; the conception was embodied in a book, called *Liber Gradalis* or *de Gradali*; this book was kept in abeyance by the British clergy for more than three hundred years, from a fear lest it should bring them into collision with the hierarchy and make their orthodoxy suspected; it came to be known and read in the second half of the twelfth century; a French poet, Robert de Boron, who probably had not seen the book, but received information about it, was the first to embody the conception in a vernacular literary form by writing his poem of Josephe d'Arimathée; and after Boron, Walter Map and others came into the field." Mr. Arnold himself inclines to think that Walter Map, about 1170–1180, connected the story of Joseph of Arimathea "with the Grail legend and both with Arthur;" and accepts Paulin Paris' now exploded derivation of the word Graal, to the effect that "graal is a corruption of gradale or graduale, the Latin name for a liturgical collection of psalms and texts of scripture, so-called ' quod in gradibus canitur,' as the priest is passing from the epistle to the gospel side of the altar. The author of the Graal conception meant by graal, or graduale, not the sacred dish (escuelle), but the mysterious book . . . in which he finds the history of the escuelle."

The romances, in prose and verse, which constitute the Grail cycle and which were written between the appearance of the *Historia Britonum* and the death of Wolfram von Eschenbach, about 1225, are so numerous, so long, so intricate, and so similar to each other in detail and general character, that it is no wonder there has been confusion; and I am far from thinking that anything like an equilibrium of opinion concerning their order of creation is likely to be established soon. Enough has been said to account for the suddenness of the phenomena—a dozen or more romances springing up within a half century, in three, or perhaps five languages. I propose further to exhibit, with incidental criticisms, the result of the latest work, presenting first the legend in synthetic form.

Now when the products of recent inquiry are taken and weighed, the statement of this interesting case must be somewhat as follows: There existed among the Celts from pre-

Christian times a folk-tale which may be called the Great Fool story, and which has been found, in some shape or other, among nearly all the peoples of Aryan race. The hero is a boy, usually a young prince, born, or at least brought up, in a wilderness, to escape the jealousy of his dead father's rival. In some cases his father was a great hero, in others a god, and generally there have been signs and wonders indicating that the boy will grow to be a mighty warrior. He is reared by his anxious mother in innocence of worldly ways, and consequently, though powerful and courageous, appears stupid beyond measure. His chief characteristics are his simplicity, strength, boldness, awkwardness, chastity, and ignorance. By some chance, he gains knowledge of the outer world, and hastens headlong from the sheltering forest and his protesting mother. In the world, none is braver or clumsier than he, and his prowess brings him in contact with the great of the earth and with monsters. After slaying dragons and winning battles he returns to his mother and comes back again into his rights.

This outline is what has been termed the Aryan Expulsion and Return Formula.[1] Mr. Nutt claims to have found eight stories built on this model in Celtic literature alone. And he does not include the Breton tales of Morvan lez Breiz and Peronnik (although they are of the same character), because their originality has been called in question.

We know also that the Welsh possessed from time immemorial a body of legend with Arthur for its centre. Whether or not the basis of this tradition was to any considerable extent historical, the whole matter is undoubtedly Celtic. Thirdly, there exist in Irish and Gaelic folklore many references to a talismanic spear and cup, the former representing the powers of destruction, the latter the powers of healing. In Welsh literature the vessel is a magic cauldron. which brings to life dead bodies that have been thrown into it. There is no longer much question of the pagan mythological origin of all these

---

[1] See von Hahn's *Arische Aussetzung und Rückkehr Formel.*

stories. By some scholars they are even connected with other more primitive legends of Eastern origin and held to have been originally part of an ancient nature-worship.

Sensible of their mystery and antiquity, and not too careful to offer an explanation of their meaning, the Welsh bards during the Norman conquest revived these slumbering traditions, no doubt largely for the patriotic reasons I have mentioned. One is tempted to see in the story of the Great Fool, who suffers contumely for a season, only to triumph eventually, one of those political prophecies with which the bards were wont to stir up resistance to the invader.

There are three members of the Grail cycle of romances which bear a striking similarity to each other, and which have not been proved to be derived directly from any known source or to have been entirely modelled on one another, and which, in spite of many efforts to show that they are later, appear all to have originated in the latter part of the twelfth century. They have each been held to be the earliest treatment of the subject which has come down to us. They all of them pre-suppose an acquaintance with the three traditions just mentioned, and thus the opinion is justified that some poet, now forever unknown, worked this mythological material into a romance which either directly or indirectly supplied three men of three different nations with the thread of three closely-related stories. These stories are that part of the *Conte du Graal* composed by Chrestien de Troyes, about 1190, in French; the English metrical romance, *Sir Perceval*, found in the Thornton manuscript; and the Welsh mabinogi, or prose romance, *Peredur, the Son of Evrawc.* The Thornton *Sir Perceval*, a fine old poem in racy English, is accessible in the publications of the Camden Society, for which it was edited by Halliwell. The *Peredur* is also accessible to English readers in Lady Charlotte Guest's *Mabinogion.*

I will now give a summary of Chrestien's poem, which has never been translated into English. The Knight Bliocadrans is slain at a tournament given by the King of Wales and

Cornwall.   During his absence his wife has borne a son, Perceval, whom, on hearing the sad news, she takes with her to
the Waste Forest.   She warns him, to preserve him from his
father's fate, that men in iron armor are devils ; but one day,
in the joyous springtime, he comes running home to say he has
met five knights, and that they are angels and not devils.   He
is determined to follow these shining creatures.   She pleads
with him in vain.   He has learned from his new acquaint-
ances that knighthood may be won from King Arthur.   So,
in despair, she makes him a rude dress of leather and gives
him some curious and enigmatical advice, namely, that if he
meets a maiden he is to take her ring and girdle, if he can, and
kiss her if she is willing.   He fares forth boldly, leaving his
mother in a swoon, and the first of his adventures is with a
maiden whom he discovers in a tent, and from whom he wrests
kisses, ring, and girdle, as advised.   Coming to Arthur's court,
he bears himself bravely, but boorishly, and is accounted a
fool for his pains.   He sallies out, however, in pursuit of a Red
Knight who has insulted the Queen.   After slaying the Red
Knight, whose armor he dons and whose steed he mounts,
Perceval comes to the castle of an old knight, Gonemans, who
teaches him the arts and manners of a gentleman warrior, coun-
selling him especially not to be too quick to ask and answer
questions. After a series of adventures and a love passage
with Blanchefleur, Gonemans' niece, who dwells in a castle
a day's journey further on, he sets forth to seek his mother.
But he has scarcely departed when he meets two men fishing
from a boat in a river.   One of them directs him to his own
castle, whither Perceval goes alone and with some misgiving,
as it is hard to find.   Suddenly it rises before him.   He is
courteously received, clothed in scarlet, and led into a great
hall, where an old man lies upon a couch before a fire, with
four hundred men about him.   A young man enters with a
sword, on which is written that it will break only in one peril,
and that its maker alone knows.   The old man gives it to
Perceval, as a guerdon from a fair lady, his niece.   Another

attendant now advances with a bleeding lance. Two other men then enter with candlesticks, and a maiden accompanies them, bearing a shining *graal*. Another maiden carries a plate. Though all these objects are borne past him, Perceval essays not to ask concerning them, remembering Gonemans' advice. Supper is served, the graal re-enters, and Perceval still forbears to ask. After supper he is shown to his chamber.

On the morrow he finds the castle deserted and silent, and his horse waiting for him already saddled. When he rides out over the drawbridge the portcullis closes so suddenly that they are almost caught. On his journey that day he encounters a maiden mourning over a dead knight. When she hears his story she tells him that the fisher and the old man on the couch were the same; that he often fished, to forget the pain of a spear-thrust through the thighs from which he suffered, and that from this he was called the Fisher King. She asks Perceval his own name. He is ignorant of it, but she tells him he is Perceval le Gallois and should be called Perceval the Caitiff, for that if he had asked the meaning of the lance, the *graal*, and the plate, his question would have brought health to the king and other benefits. After conducting himself nobly in many more adventures, which are related with great breadth of detail, Perceval rejoins Arthur's court at Carlion (Caerleon), and is there again reproached for his backwardness in not asking the desired questions. This time his accuser is a damsel fouler to view than anything imaginable outside hell, and she comes riding into court on a yellow mule. If he had asked, the King would have recovered and reigned in peace; but now slaughter and disgrace will come upon the land, maidens will suffer shame, widows and orphans will increase, and many good knights will lose their lives.

A long section of the poem is here devoted to the career of Gauwain, a knight of Arthur's court, who finally goes forth in search of the bleeding lance. Meanwhile Perceval, who has wandered to and fro on the earth for five years, doing valiant service as a knight, but forgetful of God in his heart, meets,

one Good Friday, three knights with their ladies, all dressed
as penitents.   They rebuke Perceval for his irreligion in riding armed on that day, and convicted of his sin he hastens to
a holy hermit, to whom he confesses that he has neglected God
out of spite and grief at his failure to discover the meaning of
the *graal*.   The hermit, who turns out to be his uncle, tells
Perceval that the sin which stands between him and the knowledge of that mystery, and which binds his tongue from asking
concerning *graal* and lance, is having caused the death of his
mother by his desertion of her.   From this sin and all others
his hermit-uncle absolves him, and he rides forth new-conse-
crated to the quest.   The story here returns to Gauwain, and
Chrestien's portion breaks off suddenly.

Its Northern-French continuators wrote later, of course, and
on plans and from sources different from Chrestien's.   Enough
has been given to show how these early Grail romances treated
the young Perceval saga and the talismans.   The mabinogi and
the Thornton *Sir Perceval*, as has been said, although corres-
ponding to Chrestien's fragment, the former almost incident
for incident, cannot be proved to have been based entirely upon
it.   They bear the marks of an equal antiquity, and the Welsh
story especially is penetrated with a local and racial spirit.
Here is an episode related in nearly all the romances of the
cycle, but in none so beautifully and with such richness of detail
as in the mabinogi; I quote Lady Charlotte Guest's translation:

"And in the evening he entered a valley, and at the head of
the valley he came to a hermit's cell, and the hermit welcomed
him gladly, and there he spent the night.   And in the morning he arose, and when he went forth, behold a shower of snow
had fallen the night before, and a hawk had killed a wild fowl
in front of the cell.   And the noise of the horse scared the hawk
away, and a raven alighted upon the bird.   And Peredur (Perceval) stood, and compared the blackness of the raven and the
whiteness of the snow and the redness of the blood to the hair
of the lady that best he loved, which was blacker than jet, and
to her skin which was whiter than the snow, and to the two red

spots upon her cheeks, which were redder than the blood upon the snow appeared to be."

There is another incident in the mabinogi, which bears a striking likeness to some of the main features of the Siegfried myth in the German Heldensage. Peredur has just overcome in single combat a terrible, one-eyed "black man," the father of a beautiful maiden, whose sympathies were with the youthful knight. "'Black man,' cries Peredur, 'thou shalt have mercy provided thou tell me who thou art, and who put out thine eye.' 'Lord, I will tell thee; I lost it in fighting with the Black Serpent of the Carn. There is a mound, which is called the Mound of Mourning; and upon the mound there is a carn, and in the carn there is a serpent, and on the tail of the serpent there is a stone, and the virtues of the stone are such that whosoever should hold it in one hand, in the other he will have as much gold as he may desire.'" This monster Peredur slays, and cuts off its head. Earlier in the same mabinogi there is a very similar mention made of what is evidently the same serpent, and the fact that the incident has been thus divided goes towards proving that the author was following two originals of the same story and confounded their several relations of one event. We must suppose that at least one of the originals was obscure through age or through being in a foreign language, or else that one or both of the sources was popular tradition. The other mention of a serpent is as follows: "Peredur rode forward next day, and he traversed a vast tract of desert, in which no dwellings were. And at length he came to a habitation, mean and small. And there he heard that there was a serpent that lay upon a gold ring, and suffered none to inhabit the country for seven miles around. And Peredur came to the place where he heard the serpent was. And angrily, furiously, and desperately fought he with the serpent; and at last he killed it and took away the ring."

But this is the Young Siegfried myth! With a few changes of name, we have before us the old German saga of the Rhinegold! The one-eyed black man recalls Wotan, the dark, one-

eyed, blue-cloaked wanderer, of the Heldensage, the Odin of
the Edda; the serpent and ring seem unmistakably related to
the Dragon guarding the Nibelungen ring, which conferred
wealth upon its possessor; the beautiful daughter bears a fainter
resemblance to Brünhilde, and Peredur, not only here, but in
many other passages in the Celtic cycle, is closely analogous to
Siegfried. But this ought not to surprise any one who had
read attentively the story of Young Perceval and his mother
in the Forest, which already suggests the Horny Siegfried of
German poetry. There is in the mabinogi, moreover, a sword-
test similar to that imposed upon the Volsung hero. Peredur
is challenged to try his strength by cutting through an iron
staple. He twice partially succeeds, but the severed fragments
jump together again. The third time they do not unite. Compare in the Elder Edda the song of Sigurd (Siegfried) the
Slayer of Fafnir, "Sigurdbarkvidha Fafnisbana önnur," and
its repetition in the Prose Edda.

It will be seen later that the Knights of the Grail, after
eating of the food prepared by the holy vessel, became filled
with more than human knowledge. Thus to Adam and Eve
came knowledge through eating, and thus Siegfried, after tast-
ing the Dragon's blood, had power to understand the speech
of birds.

Apart from these marks of antiquity, there is something in
the style of the mabinogi which stamps it as unquestionably
Celtic in substance, if not in original conception. The following passage is notably delicate, quivering with sensitiveness to
the impressions made by nature: "And he came towards a
valley, through which ran a river; and the borders of the
valley were wooded, and on each side of the river were level
meadows. And on one side of the river he saw a flock of
white sheep, and on the other a flock of black sheep. And
whenever one of the white sheep bleated, one of the black
sheep would cross over and become white; and when one of
the black sheep bleated, one of the white sheep would cross
over, and become black. And he saw a tall tree by the side

of the river, one-half of which was in flames from the root to the top, and the other half was green and in full leaf. And nigh thereto he saw a youth sitting upon a mound, and two greyhounds, white-breasted and spotted, in leashes, lying by his side. And certain was he that he had never seen a youth of so royal a bearing as he. And in the wood opposite he heard hounds raising a herd of deer. And Peredur saluted the youth, and the youth greeted him in turn."

Whichever of these three versions may be the oldest, and no order of priority has yet been established, it seems clear that in some such shape as they present them the germs of the Legend of the Holy Grail are found. This is proved by the immaturity of the ancient elements that occur in them (the Young Perceval story, hints of the Grail, allusions to Arthur). No one would have written thus vaguely who had before him detailed accounts such as the *Queste* and Robert de Borron's trilogy, which Birch-Hirschfeld reckons as the earliest existing members of the cycle. Moreover, the mabinogi, the Thornton *Sir Perceval*, and Chrestien's poem are naive creations, very simple and antique in spirit, as compared with the other romances, which are in a tone of highly developed chivalry.

It is probable that some Norman-English compiler, during the time of interest in Welsh affairs under Henry the Second, introduced the story to the French-reading world in a version which we do not possess. This version Chrestien and the authors of the mabinogi and of *Sir Perceval* used as the chief basis for their own. There may indeed have been also an independent Latin version, as maintained by the medieval romance-writers themselves. The main feature of this original was not the *graal*, for neither the English nor the Welsh version directly mentions such a thing; it is simply the old and widespread folk-tale of the Great Fool, derived through Celtic tradition and bearing traces of its passage. There are talismans, to be sure, and there are Arthur and his court, but these features, while likewise Celtic, are evidently not the core of the romance as thus far developed. The talismans, indeed, are not mentioned in the English *Sir Perceval*.

Up to this time there has been no evidence that any Christian symbolical meaning was attached to the *graal*, beyond the fact that Perceval, as directed by the holy hermit, expected to obtain a spiritual benefit if he discovered it and the lance and asked concerning them. They are invariably spoken of with awe and veneration, but there is still a vast difference between this tone and the accents of purely Christian devotion with which readers of monkish legends are familiar. It is possible to discern a general reference to the crusades, but so indefinite that the advocates of a classical origin for these romances (and I believe there are two such advocates, the authors of the article "Romance" in the *Encyclopædia Britannica*) might as easily discover allusions to the Quest of the Golden Fleece.

It is at this stage of development that the legend is released from its local and national limitations and begins its progress around the world. Just what Chrestien understood by the word *graal* is not clear, but he evidently felt that there was in it a mysterious import, and no doubt would have developed his idea much further if he had lived to complete his poem. That he had no precise conception of its meaning and yet wished to appear to have, is evident from his equivocal allusions to it.

The meaning of the word *graal* has been the subject of much discussion. The romance writers themselves derived it from the French verb *agréer*, 'to please,' or directly from the Latin adjective *gratus*, and frequently spelled it *gréaus*. It seems to me that their allusions to this etymology are not merely in the nature of puns, but were intended seriously; it is thus plain that they did not know the real meaning of the word. It is in fact from the Low Latin *gradale*, from a diminutive, *cratella*, of the Latin *cratera*, sometimes *craterra*, Greek $\kappa\rho\alpha\tau\dot{\eta}\rho$ or $\kappa\rho\alpha\tau\eta\rho\acute{\iota}\alpha$, 'a mixing-bowl.' There is no reason whatever for accepting the explanation, so often put forward, that *san greal* is derived from *sang real*, the royal blood. For one thing, the word *graal* occurs too often and too early out of connection with the *san*. A most interesting, but somewhat frail supposition, is that which connects *gradale*, 'a bowl,' with *gradale* or *graduale*, 'a mass-book' containing responses for the priest or choir *in gradibus*. Paulin Paris, whose acceptance of this view is responsible for its general adoption, bases his theory on the following passage from the chronicle of Helinandus, a Cistercian monk in the abbey of Froidmond, in the diocese of Beauvais. The chronicle runs down to 1209 and must therefore have been completed not earlier than that year: Anno 717. Hoc tempore, cuidam eremitae monstrata est mirabilis quaedam visio per Angelum, de sancto Josepho, decurione nobili, qui corpus Domini deposuit de cruce ; et de catino illo vel paropside in quo Dominus coenavit cum discipulis suis ; de qua ab eodem eremita descripta est historia quae dicitur *Gradal.* Gradalis autem vel Gradale dicitur gallicè scutella lata et aliquantulum profunda in qua pretiosae dapes, cum suo jure (in their juice) divitibus solent apponi, et dicitur nomine *Graal.* . . Hanc historiam latinè scriptam invenire non potui ; sed tantum gallicè scripta habetur a quibusdam proceribus ; nec facilè, ut aiunt, tota inveniri potest. Hanc autem nondum potui ad legendum sedulo ab aliquo impetrare.[1]

Chrestien's poem contains 10,601 verses. It was continued to verse 34,934 by Gautier de Doulens, who probably took up the work soon after Chrestien's death. In his portion very little light is thrown upon the meaning and origin of the *graal*, which, however, has now become manifestly the central feature of the poem. We know nothing about this Gautier except what the manuscripts of his poem themselves tell us, and they merely declare that he was its author, in the following passage, verses 33,755–8 (Potvin's edition) :

> Gautiers de Doulens, qui l'estore,
> Nos a mis avant en memore,
> dist et conte que Perchevaus
> li bons chevaliers, li loiaus.

[1] For a more minute account of what has been written about the etymology of the word graal, see Skeat's preface, p. xxxvi, to the Early English Text Society's edition of *Joseph of Arimathie.*

3

Doulens is near Amiens, and the dialect is Picard.   The *Conte du Graal* had other continuators, but they were considerably later (1216–1225), and there are passages even in the earlier portions, those attributed to Chrestien and Gautier, which are considered by both Birch-Hirschfeld and Nutt to be late interpolations.   The latter says of one of these "interpolations" (the passage found in the Berne MS. and incorporated in Gautier's section): "The existence of this fragment shows the necessity of collating all the MSS. of the *Conte du Graal* and the impossibility of arriving at definite conclusions respecting the growth of the work before this is done. . . . . It is hopeless, in the present state of knowledge, to do more than map out approximately the leading sections of the work."

At some point in the period to which Chrestien's poem is assigned (1170–1212), there appeared the earliest versions we possess of a Christian legend which was destined soon to be combined and inextricably complicated with the story of Young Perceval, the talismans, and Arthur's court.   One of these versions is found interpolated, in several manuscripts, between Chrestien's and Gautier's sections of the *Conte du Graal.*   The substance of it is as follows (I quote Nutt's summary): "Joseph of Barimacie[1] had a dish made; with it he caught the blood running from the Saviour's body as it hung on the Cross; he afterward begged the body of Pilate; for the devotion showed the Grail he was denounced to the Jews, thrown into prison, delivered thence by the Lord, exiled together with the sister of Nicodemus, who had an image of the Lord.   Joseph and his companions came to the promised land, the White Isle, a part of England.   There they warred against them of the land. When Joseph was short of food he prayed to the Creator to send him the Grail wherein he had gathered the holy blood, after which to them that sat at table the Grail brought bread and wine and meat in plenty.   At his death Joseph begged the

---

[1] *Joseph of Arimathia.* Nutt remarks that the form Barimacie bears witness to a Latin original, being corrupted evidently from *ab Arimathia.*

Grail might remain with his seed, and thus it was that no one, of however high condition, might see it save he was of Joseph's blood. The Rich Fisher was of that kin, and so was Grelogue-vaus, from whom came Perceval." The date of this passage cannot be even approximately ascertained; but it is not the only version of the legend. It is evident from the increased attention Gautier pays to the *graal* that he was acquainted with some such account. Besides, he tells that the *gréaus* was given by the King of kings as he hung on the Cross, and that "the devil may not lead astray any man on the same day he sees it."

But in addition to these witnesses we have a detailed poem by Robert de Borron (a reference he makes to his lord, Walter of Montbeliard, fixes its date between 1170 and 1212) on the early history of the Grail. Here for the first time we enter an atmosphere apparently of prevailingly Christian tone. Beginning with Borron's poem, we have many accounts of the origin, the wanderings, the miracles, and the spiritual significance of the Grail. They agree substantially to this effect: The Grail was the vessel used by Christ at the Last Supper, obtained from Pilate by Joseph of Arimathia, who received in it the blood from Christ's wounds when our Lord's body was taken from the Cross. During a long captivity which he suffered for his fidelity, Joseph was fed and comforted by the holy vessel, which came to him in his prison, filling it with glorious light. Upon his release Joseph brought the sacred emblem to England, where he or his descendants founded the British church. It would remain in the keeping of Joseph's family until a chosen knight should come, to be its king and guardian. Some versions relate that the Grail was brought to England by Brons, Joseph's brother-in-law; others that Joseph, after bringing it to England himself, confided it to Brons.

Somewhere about this time, but the dates and order are matter of vexed discussion, were written the prose romances, the *Queste del Saint Graal* and the *Grand Saint Graal*. Robert de Borron's poetical romance was originally in three parts,

Joseph d'Arimathie, Merlin, Perceval. Of the first part we
possess nearly all, of the second the beginning; the third is
lost; but of the first two parts and perhaps of all three, there
have come down to us versions in prose. Furthermore, we
have another independent prose version, entitled *Perceval le
Gallois*, the German poetical version *Parzival*, of Wolfram von
Eschenbach, and Heinrich von dem Türlin's *Diu Crône*, not
to mention in this connection mere fragments, variants, and
translations.

The incidents of the Grail's "early history" are, at first
blush, similar in character to those of most other monkish
legends. They furnish a good illustration of how far, at that
time, the canon of the New Testament scriptures was from
being established, and with how little compunction medieval
religious writers sometimes mingled their own inventions with
the sacred narratives. Statements of canonical and apocryphal
books are not distinguished from mouth to mouth tradition or
from sheer fiction. The apocryphal authority most used is the
Evangelium Nicodemi, which was known and popular in England several centuries before it is mentioned by any continental
writer except Gregory of Tours. The apocryphal narrative of
Joseph was also employed, and the *Vindicta Salvatoris*. The
accounts of the early history of the Grail are in all but two
romances bound up with a history of the quest, based upon
stories of Perceval's youth, the talismans, and Arthur's court,
which we have seen are of Celtic pagan origin.

The *Queste del Saint Graal*, a prose romance attributed in
the manuscripts themselves to Walter Map, and found generally in the same manuscripts with the *Lancelot* and the *Mort
Artur*, is plainly of secondary or tertiary construction, although
dating from the period 1190–1200, and written without knowledge of Borron's poem. Birch-Hirschfeld has done what he
could to shake the statement that Walter Map was its author.
I am glad to believe that he has not succeeded. It is a great
satisfaction to have in the cycle at least one author about whose
life and character we possess some outside knowledge. Walter

Map was born before 1143 and died in 1210. He was one of the most versatile writers of his day, a prominent courtier under Henry the Second and perhaps also under Richard and John, and one of the highest dignitaries of the English church. Having been educated at the University of Paris, he was several times chosen to fill important political and ecclesiastical posts on the Continent. His writings are in French and Latin, although he was an Englishman, and probably a native of the Welsh border. His most celebrated Latin work, *De Nugis Ourialium*, is a book of personal reminiscences and miscellaneous gossip, and shows the immense range of his experience and his curiosity in many fields of literary attainment. His long sojourns in France, his intellectual eminence, and the fact that he was born just when and where he was, make possible his having been able at least to know all the legends and romances upon which the *Queste del Saint Graal* is based, and to conceive the idea of writing a book which should combine them and transfuse them with new spiritual significance.

Birch-Hirschfeld's chief argument against his authorship is that he could not have had time, in his busy life of civil and ecclesiastical politics, to compose the vast romances which call themselves his. Yet precisely in his travels in France and England, and in his diplomatic activity, would he have found material for his works, which are chiefly the piling up of adventure upon adventure, with very little attempt at coördination. If a learned and travelled man had kept account of all the stories of chivalry that fell under his notice, he might quickly and easily have strung them together in his old age. Mr. Skeat, in the preface to his edition of the Vernon MS. *Joseph of Arimathia*, printed for the Early English Text Society in 1871, takes a view, however, that is entirely too radical, especially as it is unsupported by proofs, when he says: "The Lancelot of Chrestien de Troyes has been proved conclusively by a Flemish scholar, W. J. A. Jonckbloet, to have been founded upon the Lancelot of Walter Map; and in like manner I suppose that Chrestien borrowed his Perceval le Gallois from

Map also, in a great measure. I can see no reason why we may
not assume Walter Map's romance, of which the original Latin
version is lost, to have been the real original from which all
the rest were more or less imitated."   He quotes with appro-
bation Professor Morley's exclamation :   " Where was there
an author able to invent it and to write it with a talent so 'pro-
digious,' except Walter Map, to whom alone, and to whom
always, positively, it has been ascribed?"   Again Mr. Skeat
says : " The original Latin text by Walter Map being lost, we
are left to conjecture what it was like from the various translations and imitations of it.   And first, there is the Romance in
French verse, as composed by Robert de Boron about A. D.
1170."   Whether Map learned from Borron or Borron from
Map, or both, as is more likely, from common sources, the
Frenchman's poem and the Englishman's *Queste* are the earliest
and best presentations of the Early History, or Christian legend,
of the Grail.   The elements of this legend, though old enough,
far older doubtless than any version we possess, can hardly compare in antiquity with the pagan mythological sources from
which sprang the story of Young Perceval.

It would seem a difficult task to show how the two streams,
thus starting far apart, one pagan and the other Christian,
flowed together, blending into the great spiritual legend of
which the one transcendent outcome is the Grail, the symbol
of Christ's visible presence and the object of the purest human
aspiration.   It is indeed a problem which has taxed and baffled
the minds of many scholars.   Only of very recent years has
a solution been proposed which in a measure satisfies the re-
quirements of probability and is in accord with the great mass
of other phenomena in comparative literature.   This triumph
was reserved for students of specifically Celtic mythology and
folk-lore.   If their conclusions appear disappointing to those
who would fain discover a Christian origin for the noblest of
medieval legends, on the other hand they must prove gratify-
ing to all lovers of consistency.   What these Celtic scholars
have done is no less than to show that the real origin of the

early history as well as of the quest is Celtic and pagan ! Mr. Nutt, whose researches seem to have been inspired and assisted by J. F. Campbell's *Popular Tales of the West Highlands*, finds in Bran, the hero of an Irish myth, " the starting-point of the Christian transformation of the legend." Brons is no other than Bran, who, in Celtic tradition, is "ruler of the other world," of Avalon, the land of the blessed, beyond the western sea, whither the choicest heroes go questing. In the Christian legend the seat of Brons' influence, where he began the conversion of the Britons, is Glastonbury, which was one of the first centres of Christian influence in Britain. Mr. Nutt asks : " Is it too rash a conjecture that the Christian church may have taken the place of some Celtic temple or holy spot specially dedicated to the cult of the dead and of that Lord of the Shades from which the Celts feigned their descent? "

This is indeed a bold speculation, particularly when we consider the earliness of Borron's poem and the *Queste del Saint Graal*, and their thorough Christian character, and remember also the rapidity with which all subsequent writers accepted the Christian-legendary account. I do not see either why Mr. Nutt should give so little weight to the early influence of the *Evangelium Nicodemi*. His view, however, is consistent with the shrewd proposition which he assumes in starting, but happily does not lay too much stress upon, viz : that the tendency in medieval literature is from the racial-heathen towards the Christian-legendary. However valuable this principle, and by the analogy of Scandinavian and German literatures it is most excellent, the force of Mr. Nutt's argument depends entirely upon the character of the Celtic folk-stories to which he and Professor Rhŷs, who follows him enthusiastically, refer. The whole field is open only to them and other learned Celtic students like them ; but they have provided us samples enough to furnish a judgment, and their conclusions on this head must be regarded as final in the present state of knowledge.

We have now reached the following results respecting the ultimate sources of the Holy Grail legend : First, the source whence sprang the most beautiful feature, the feature which was the most prominent one in early versions, is the Young Perceval folk-tale. This story, as found among nearly all peoples of Aryan race, is called the Expulsion and Return formula, and has been connected by many recent investigators with a solar myth, as representing the setting and rising of the sun, or a secular myth, as representing the departure and return of spring. While the formula is almost universal, the particular variety in this case is Celtic. Secondly, the poets of the Holy Grail cycle availed themselves of the legends about Merlin and Arthur and other figures of Celtic mythology which were prominent in the twelfth century. These legends had been in part revived, in part forged, in part new created, and all for a political reason which the history of Wales makes sufficiently clear. Thirdly, there exist, even in our earliest versions, mysterious and pregnant allusions to certain objects, either pagan talismans or Christian relics; and in the later growth of the legend it is to these that a predominating development is given. The most recent phase of study has been the discussion of the complicated problem here presented: Are these objects in their remotest origin pagan or Christian? Do they represent some ancient Druidical usage and was the knowledge of them kept alive through Celtic tradition; or were they of monkish creation, the outgrowth of the scriptural and apocryphal and legendary accounts of the early Christian church?

Now it is evident that if the Christian-origin hypothesis were true we should find the sacred objects treated as Christian symbols in the earliest as well as the latest versions we possess. But such is not the case, unless I am wrong in claiming an earlier date for Chrestien's poem, the mabinogi, and the Thornton *Sir Perceval* than for the works of Robert Borron and Walter Map. In the Thornton *Sir Perceval* there is no mention whatever of sword, lance, spear, dish, *graal*, or salver, whether as Christian relics or as pagan talismans. In Chrestien's portion of the *Conte du Graal* the mention is not such as to justify the Christian-origin hypothesis. Mysterious objects are alluded to in such a way as to indicate that the author did not understand their nature or significance, or else did not wish yet to inform his readers on these points. This has been explained by saying that Chrestien was reserving this information for the conclusion of his poem, when it was to be introduced with some effect of surprise. But Gautier, who continued Chrestien's poem almost immediately and probably had access to the same material as Chrestien, is only a little more definite than he, and in the meanwhile the transformation is conceded to have begun. In the mabinogi a bleeding spear and a salver containing a man's head are introduced, but with no hint of their being relics of Christ's passion. Furthermore, Wolfram, who based his poem largely on Chrestien's, states explicitly that he had another source as well, the now lost Kiot. I think Wolfram's declaration worthy of credence, although that is a very bold thing to do, since most of his recent critics, and the best of them, at that, have denied the existence of this Kiot and given the lie to that most worthy and Christian knight, Wolfram von Eschenbach, who proudly asserted that he was no mere literary man. Now Wolfram, while penetrated to the heart with the most fervent Christian mysticism and displaying everywhere his love of allegory and his faith in God's special interferences, does nowhere regard the *graal* as the vessel which received Christ's blood. Its significance for him is indeed religious, but he has evidently never heard of the origin ascribed to it by the authors of the *Joseph*, the *Queste del Saint Graal*, and the *Grand Saint Graal*, by Robert de Borron and Walter Map, and all the writers who adopt the legendary story.

In Wolfram's *Parzival* the *graal* is a precious stone, yielding bounteous store of food and drink ; to it, every passion week, flutters down from heaven a dove, which places upon it a holy wafer. At the fall of the rebellious angels it was received from God by Titurel and his dynasty, and preserved by them in Montsalvat, the Grail Castle. It chooses its own guardians, a sacred knighthood, vowed to virginity, all except their king.

Anfortas, the maimed king, was wounded not more in body than in soul, "for having taken up arms in the cause of worldly and unlawful love." Now if Wolfram had any other model besides Chrestien, and he says he had Kiot, this ignorance of his shows that another and still older writer was also ignorant of the Joseph legend. Wolfram, discontented with Chrestien's lack of moral and religious profundity, protests against being considered an imitator of his, and informs us that his model was Kiot the Provençal (or Kiot of Provins). There is absolutely no trace of such a poet except in Wolfram. Spanish and Provençal literatures have been searched through in vain for evidence of the existence in medieval Provençal of a Grail romance. But Wolfram's assertions are too explicit to be lightly passed over. Let us take his words in evidence.

In *Parzival*, 452, 29, speaking of the pious Trevrezent, a hermit whom the hero encounters on his travels:

> an dem ervert nu Parzivâl
> diu verholnen mære umben grâl.
> Swer mich dervon ê frâgte
> unt drumbe mit mir bâgte,
> ob ichs im niht sagte,
> umprîs der dran bejagte.
> mich batez helen Kyôt,
> wand im diu âventiure gebôt
> daz es immer man gedæhte,
> ê ez d'âventiure bræhte
> mit worten an der mæhre gruoz
> daz man dervon doch sprechen muoz.
> Kyôt der meister wol bekant
> ze Dôlet verworfen ligen vant
> in heidenischer schrifte
> dirre âventiure gestifte.
> der karakter â b c
> muoser hân gelernet ê,
> ân den list von negrômanzî.
> es half daz im der touf was bî:
> anders waer diz maer noch unvernumn.
> kein heidensch list möht uns gefrumn
> ze künden umbes grâles art,
> wie man sîner tougen inne wart.

ein heiden Flegetânîs
bejagte an künste hôhen prîs.
der selbe fisêôn
was gehorn von Salmôn,
ûz israhêlscher sippe erzilt
von alter her, unz unser schilt
der touf wart fürz hellefiur.
der schreip vons grâles âventiur.
Er was ein heiden vaterhalp
Flegetânîs, der an ein kalp
bette als op ez wær sîn got.
wie mac der tievel selhen spot
gefüegen an sô wîser diet,
daz si niht scheidet ode schiet
dâ von der treit die böhsten haut
unt dem elliu wunder sint bekant?
    Flegetânîs der heiden
kunde uns wol bescheiden
ieslîches sternen binganc
unt sîner künfte widerwanc;
wie lange ieslîcher umbe gêt,
ê er wider an sîn zil gestêt.
mit der sternen umbereise vart
ist gepüfel aller menschlier art.
Flegetânîs der heiden sach,
dâ von er blûweclîche sprach,
im gestirn mit sînen ougen
verholenbæriu tougen.
er jach, es hiez ein dinc der grâl:
des namen las er sunder twâl
inme gestirne, wie der hiez.
'ein schar in ûf der erden liez:
diu fuor ûf über die sterne hôch.
op die ir unschult wider zôch,
sît muoz sîn pflegn getouftiu fruht
mit alsô kiuschlîcher zuht:
diu menscheit ist immer wert,
der zuo dem grâle wirt gegert.'
    Sus schreip dervon Flegetânîs.
Kyôt der meister wîs
diz mære begunde suochen
in latînschen buochen,
wâ gewesen wære
ein volc dâ zuo gebære
daz ez des grâles pflæge

> unt der kiusche sich bewæge.
> er las der lande chrônicá
> ze Britâne unt anderswâ,
> ze Francrîche unt in Yrlant:
> ze Anschouwe er diu mære vant.
> er las von Mazadân
> mit wârheite sunder wân:
> umb allez sîn geslehte
> stuont dâ geschriben rehte,
> unt anderhalp wie Tyturel
> unt des sun Frimutel
> den grâl bræht ûf Amfortas,
> des swester Herzeloyde was,
> bî der Gahmuret ein kint
> gewan, des disiu mære sint.[1]

It is scarcely likely that Wolfram could read Provençal, or indeed that Kiot wrote in that language.   It is probable that he used a Northern French dialect, though it is not necessary to suppose that the chronicle of Anjou really did furnish him anything about the Grail.   The fact that he is called Kiot the Provençal would indicate that he did *not* live in Provence; else why should his nationality be emphasized?   Without denying that this story about Flegetanis and Kiot has many elements of the fictitious, for the most part it seems to me credible enough.   Wolfram is almost as serious and reliable as Dante. Who would think of disbelieving the Italian poet's downright and oft-repeated assertions?   And Wolfram insists on Kiot. I am not, however, insusceptible to the force of Birch-Hirschfeld's argument that Wolfram, having borrowed wholesale from Chrestien, and wishing to draw attention from that fact, pretended to have a recondite source in Kiot, of whom no trace exists, and made as little mention of Chrestien as possible.   I will admit further that there occurs to me, in support of Birch-Hirschfeld's theory, a reason which I have never seen advanced, namely that Wolfram has not always wrought with that sad sincerity becoming to a medieval religious poet, but indulges on every opportunity in his peculiar humor; his assertion that

---

[1] I have translated this important and interesting passage in Appendix A.

he could not read and was no mere literary man may be taken
as an example, for it is preposterous to suppose that he was
illiterate, and the connection in which the remark occurs is full
of repartee with imaginary readers.   But just because of these
readers, he could not have been romancing in so serious a matter
as the Kiot authorship, for he evidently wrote in anticipation of
being read by court people of his own acquaintance, who would
be sure to bring him to book for his statements, as he says certain
ladies had done once before.

The Anglo-Norman writers of the Holy Grail cycle also
insist on certain Latin books, whose existence Mr. Nutt seems
to scoff at; and I see no reason to deny that there may have
been versions in Latin, or in French either, which have been
lost.[1] Indeed the inconsistency, coupled with similarity, of the
versions we do possess points irresistibly to such a conclusion.
There is no use in making the problem harder than it is by
shutting ourselves up with the versions we have and trying to
make them fit together, when they absolutely will not fit. If
ever there was room for the respectful consideration of unknown
quantities it is here. If ever speculation was justifiable, besides
being delightful, it is also here.

Whatever its origin, the Legend of the Holy Grail speedily
acquired a tone of Christian mysticism. The Grail itself, which
was so little alluded to at first, grew to a figure of paramount
importance. An amazing number of versions sprang up within
a single half-century. Looking at the legend as a supernatural
being may be supposed to regard all mundane phenomena,—
that is independently of the limitations and order of time, it
must be admitted that its root and life, its fruit, its purpose, its
essential principle, its promise for the future, is the beautiful
idea of a spiritual knighthood, seeking not earthly love and
favor, but the sacred emblem of our Saviour's sacrifice, the

---

[1] Again I plead for more faith in MS. statements. MS. 2,455 Bibl. Nat.
(of the *Grand Saint Graal*) says: Or dist li contes qui est estrais de toutes
les ystoires, si come Robers de Borons le translatoit de latin en romans, à
l'ayde de maistre Gautier Map.

miraculous vessel of his immanent grace, the medium of his
bounty.   The lapse of ages has enabled us to look backward
with somewhat of supernatural freedom from ordinary logic;
and we may, without great violence to historical facts, transfer
the final cause to the position of the formal cause, and declare
that in this transcendental sense Tennyson and Wagner are
nearer the truth than Mr. Nutt and Professor Rhŷs. Yet from
an every-day point of view the latter, it appears to me, have
given us at last a sound theory as to the ultimate sources of
the legend.

The embodiment of the legend is in the following versions,
which have come down to us. I have endeavored to arrange
them as nearly as possible in chronological order, that being,
however, a matter of much uncertainty. Mr. Nutt's work, the
most elaborate treatment of the subject, and based on vast
research, and conducted with judgment and fairness, affords
authority for most of the table.

1. Chrestien's portion of the *Conte du Graal.*   The *Conte
du Graal* is a poem containing over 60,000 verses, of which
Chrestien de Troyes, a celebrated Northern French poet, wrote
10,600.   Ch. Potvin printed, for the first time, 45,379 verses,
from a MS. in the library of Mons, Belgium : *Le Conte du
Graal,* 6 vols., 8vo. ; Mons, 1866–71. A complete edition of
Chrestien's works is now being edited by Foerster. Of this
three volumes have already appeared, containing the *Chevalier
au Lyon* and the *Erec et Enide;* Halle, 1890. Chrestien dedi-
cates his poem to Count Philip of Flanders, who *li bailla le
livre,* gave him the book, upon which it is based. Nutt and
Birch-Hirschfeld agree in supposing, from references to Count
Philip, that the work was begun about 1189. Three of the
continuators of the poem name themselves and claim their share
of credit for it; one of them, Gerbert, even states expressly that
Chrestien was prevented by death from proceeding with it:

ce nous dist Chrestiens de Troyes
qui de Percheval comencha
mais la mors qui l'adevancha
ne li laissa pas traire affin.

2. The mabinogi of *Peredur ab Evrawc*, as already explained, though probably written later than Chrestien's fragment, is not modelled on it necessarily, and is at least equally ancient in conception and material. It is a Welsh prose romance found in MSS. of the end of the thirteenth century, but particularly in the Red Book of Hergest, a MS. of the end of the fourteenth, preserved in the library of Jesus College, Oxford, from which it was printed, in 1838, by Lady Charlotte Guest, in her English translation of the *Mabinogion*.

3. *Sir Perceval of Galles*, an old English poem, first printed by Halliwell for the Camden Society, in 1844, from the Thornton MS. of about 1440, bears much the same relation to Chrestien's fragment and to the mabinogi that they bear to each other. The Thornton MS. is thought to be a very late copy.

4. Gautier's portion of the *Conte du Graal* (verses 10,601–34,934) was probably written shortly after Chrestien's death. The MSS. differ as to Gautier's full name, but probably it was Gautier de Doulens (a small town in Picardy, near Amiens). He mentions himself in verse 33,755.

5. The introduction to Chrestien's poem, though purporting to be by him, is evidently of later origin than the next 10,600 lines. It lays great stress on the grail and lance and on the Rich Fisher, though not generally in such a way as to imply a knowledge of the Christian legend, but rather in the full spirit of Celtic pagan folk-lore. There is one reference, however, which proves that the author, whoever he was, had begun to connect the Druidical symbols with Christian relics. The supposed discovery of the lance with which the Roman soldier pierced the side of Jesus was one of the great sensations of the first crusade. The story as told in Gibbon, chapter 58, is well known. The pseudo-Chrestien introduction relates how the court of the Rich Fisher was entertained with seven tales, of which the seventh and most pleasing " tells of the lance wherewith Longis pierced the side of the king of holy Majesty."

6. Robert de Borron's trilogy in French verse, *Joseph, Merlin, Perceval*, of which we have the *Joseph* and part of the *Merlin*,

was written probably a good while before the close of the
twelfth century.   It bears the signature of genius, and one is
not tempted to seek for other "sources" than the author's
originality, except in so far as we know he must have used
traditions which had long before grown out of the canonical
and apocryphal gospels.   Borron's poem breathes a spirit of
profoundest mysticism.   For him all incidents of his story
are fraught with a divine intention, pointing to the spiritual
reign of Christ.   Almost everything he mentions is typical of
some religious doctrine.   Ordinarily in literary criticism it is
unsafe to yield to a temptation to seek cryptic meanings; in
medieval poetry of a religious character, it is necessary to
exercise the speculative and sympathetic faculties.   Borron
connects the contemplation of the Grail with the celebration
of the Sacrament of the Supper, and the Sacrament in turn
typifies the manner and instruments of Christ's death.   " No
Sacrament shall ever be celebrated but Joseph shall be remembered.   The bread and wine are Christ's flesh and blood, the
tomb is the Altar; the grave-cloth the Corporal, the vessel
wherein the blood was put shall be called Chalice, the cup-
platter signifies the tombstone.   All who see Joseph's vessel
shall be of Christ's company, have fulfilment of their heart's
wish and joy eternal."   But with one side of the matter Borron
was not so well acquainted, and this is of importance for us.
He himself declares :

Je n'ose parler ne retraire,
Ne je ne le porroie faire,
(Neis se je feire le voloie)
Se je le grant livre n'aveie
Où les estoires sont escrites,
Par les grans clercs feites et dites.
Là sont li grant secré escrit
Qu'on nomme le Graal.

"I dare not speak of nor repeat [Joseph's secret], and not
even if I wished to do it could I do it, without having the
great book in which the stories are written, made, and told

by the great clerks. Therein are set forth the great secrets which are called the Grail." This is the sense in which Paulin Paris translates *se je le grant livre n'aveie.* Mr. Skeat, on p. xxxv of his preface to *The English Alliterative Poem Joseph of Arimathie,* published for the English Text Society, objects to this rendering, and Mr. Nutt agrees with him, translating the sentence thus : "I dare not, nor could not, tell this but that I had the great book, &c.," concluding of course that he *had* the book, whereas the inference from the former translation is that Robert de Borron believed in the existence of the *grand livre latin,* but did *not* have it under his eyes. Among the legends employed is that of St. Veronica, under the name of Verrine, who "wiped Christ's face and thus got the likeness of Him." The Holy Grail is called *Graal* because it is agreeable to all who see it. A significant feature is that Alain is commanded " to take charge of his brethren and sisters and go westwards," to Avaron, which can be nothing else than Avalon, the Elysian Fields of Druidical mythology. At the close of the *Merlin* occur the words : " And I, Robert of Borron, writer of this book, may not speak longer of Arthur till I have told of Alain, son of Brons, and how the woes of Britain were caused ; and as the book tells so must I what man Alain was, and what life he led, and of his seed and their life. And when I have spoken of these things I will tell again of Arthur." We perceive the author's intention of connecting the first Christian church in Jerusalem with the church of Britain. The unique MS. is in the Bibliothèque nationale, and contains 4,018 verses, of which 3,514 constitute the *Joseph.* It has been printed by Furnivall for the Roxburghe Club, in two volumes, London, 1861–63. The poem is often called the *Petit Saint Graal.* Nutt holds that it remained unknown for many years after its composition, since he finds no trace of its influence on romances of later date. Birch-Hirschfeld, believing he finds evidence of its influence even in the *Conte du Graal,* makes it the original member of the cycle, thus setting up a theory utterly opposed to the one we have followed.

4

7. The interpolation already noted and summarized, occurring in several MSS. of the *Conte du Graal*, in the midst of Gautier's portion. This was evidently written some time later than Gautier's portion and inserted into his account to give a representation of the Christian legend, which had by this time made credit for itself as the true and acceptable early history of the mysterious symbols.

8. An independent ending of Gautier's portion, found in the Berne MS., concluding with the following statements (I quote Nutt's summary): "The Fisher King is father to Alain le Gros, husband to Enigeus, sister to the Joseph who, when Christ's body was taken down from the Cross, had it from Pilate as a reward for his services. Joseph had the vessel prepared to catch in it the blood from the body; it was the same Jesus had made the Sacrament in, on the Thursday before. The Fisher King dies on the third day and Perceval reigns in his stead." The author of this fragment must have been acquainted with Borron's poem.

9. The *Queste del Saint Graal*, a French prose romance, was printed for the Roxburghe Club, London, 1864, by Furnivall. Although Walter Map's authorship of it is denied by high authority, we have seen that the MSS. claim him and that there is no sufficient reason to doubt that he wrote it. A Welsh version exists, which though differing in many particulars from any hitherto discovered French MS., appears to be a translation of the *Queste*. This Welsh version was printed, with a translation, by the Rev. Robert Williams, from a MS. of the fifteenth century: *Y Seint Graal*, London, 1876.

10. The *Grand Saint Graal*, a French prose romance, printed by Furnivall. The Early English Text Society has published an English metrical version based on this French original, by Herry Lonelich, of about the middle of the fifteenth century. Both Birch-Hirschfeld and Nutt, in spite of a hint in the MS. which might be taken as an ascription of it to Robert de Borron, declare that the authorship is unknown. There is contemporary evidence (the reference to it by Helindandus)

that this romance was known before 1204. Nutt holds that our version of the *Grand Saint Graal* is the result of incorporating an original of that name, now lost, with Borron's poem.

11. Manessier, a Northern French poet, under the patronage of "Jehanne la Comtesse, qu'est de Flandre dame et mestresse," took up the *Conte du Graal* at line 34,934 and finished it at line 45,379. Jehanne was sole ruler of Flanders between 1214 and 1227.

12. Another conclusion of the *Conte du Graal* is by Gerbert. Birch-Hirschfeld maintains that this was Gerbert de Montreuil, author of the *Roman de la Violette*, and furthermore that the 15,000 lines, more or less, here employed were part of a complete work of his, which was mutilated to furnish an ending to the work of Chrestien and Gautier.

13. Prose adaptations of Borron's trilogy. Their date is uncertain, but they were probably written in the first quarter of the thirteenth century. Nutt calls the prose romance of *Perceval* (the Didot-Perceval) a sequel to Borron's poem, made under the influence of the *Conte du Graal* and the *Queste*, or of material on which they are based, and maintains that it is later than all the other members of the cycle, and cannot therefore be used to prove that the third member of Borron's trilogy was of such and such a character.

14. The *Parzival* of Wolfram von Eschenbach is preserved in numerous complete and well-authenticated MSS. It has been twice translated from the Middle High German original into Modern German verse, by San Marte and later by Simrock. Wolfram was a Bavarian and lived probably between 1170 and 1220. Wolfram's complete works have been published in a critical edition by Karl Lachmann, Berlin, 1879 (fourth edition).

15. *Perceval le Gallois*, a French prose romance, is held by all critics to be of late origin, probably about 1225. There is an ancient Welsh translation of it, representing a text different from any we possess.

16. *Diu Crône*, by Heinrich von dem Türlin, another ancient German version, is subsequent to *Parzival* and based on it.

17. Ancient translations: a translation of the *Conte du Graal*
into Flemish verse, begun by Penninc and finished, in 1350, by
Peter Vorstaert; another of the same in Icelandic, preserved
in the Royal Library of Stockholm. There is also in Icelandic
an ancient short compilation based on the *Conte du Graal.*

18. The *Morte Darthur*, of Sir Thomas Malory, printed by
Caxton, in 1485, has been the medium through which the
English-speaking race has derived most of its knowledge of the
Arthurian romances, including the story of the Grail. It has
grown out from the obscurer and duller versions of the earlier
age and by its own popularity doomed them to long oblivion.
The English poets, and especially Tennyson, have drawn rich
stores from it. Caxton said that Malory took his matter "out
of certain books of French and reduced it into English."
Nevertheless he cannot be denied great originality, both for
substance and arrangement, and his style alone, which has at
all times received praise, would mark him as no mere compiler.
The editio princeps has been critically studied and republished
in superb form, with a learned introduction, by H. O. Sommer,
3 vols., London, 1891. The bibliographical notes are of great
value. Malory, who probably completed his work about 1470,
is, with respect to his attitude towards the Grail material, the
first of a new class of writers, those who employ it freely,
though reverently, as substance for original creations, modern
in form and spirit. Not only Tennyson, but Spenser, Swin-
burne, William Morris, Matthew Arnold, R. S. Hawker, and
half a dozen other English poets have essayed this theme of
the Grail quest, or the kindred themes of Arthur's kingship,
Lancelot's sin, and the luxurious woe of Tristram and Iseult.
Mr. Sommer bears witness that the vitality and popularity of
the Arthurian romances is, however, due to their internal connection with the legend of the Holy Grail. "What chivalry,
with all its warlike prowess, was unable to effect by itself, was
achieved by chivalry blended with Christianity. As long as
Arthur's knights vowed themselves solely to worldly adventures, they were like ordinary men; but when they entered upon

the quest of the Holy Grail, the search for the supernatural, the struggle for the spiritual stamped upon them immortality."

At no time since the thirteenth century have more contributions been made to the legend of the Grail than in our own time, a time profoundly in sympathy with that earlier age. The works of Tennyson and Wagner, while in so far original that they present the most modern conceptions of chivalry, morality, and religion, are yet legitimate and generic developments of the medieval material. The text of Richard Wagner's music-drama *Parsifal* is based on Wolfram. There could be no better preparation for the study of how Wolfram himself treated Chrestien's poem or Malory adapted the matter found in his " French books,'[1] than a consideration of the way in which this most modern of poets chose what suited the demands of his imperious purpose. Mr. H. E. Krehbiel, in his delightful *Studies in the Wagnerian Drama*, has traced for English readers, but only too briefly, the genesis of Wagner's conception : how he, at an early point in his career, outlined a tragedy, *Jesus of Nazareth*, and eight years later, in 1856, another, *The Victors*, from a Buddhistic legend. Wagner himself has told us that at this time his mind was possessed by the philosophy of Schopenhauer. The theme of *The Victors* was to be abnegation, the voluntary annihilation of life. The love of the hero and heroine, Prakriti and Ananda, was to be surrendered at the instance of Buddha, and they were to retire from the world and live in celibacy. In this tone of mind, which was in fact the dominating mood of his art-life, Wagner composed *Tristan und Isolde ;* this underlying idea gave birth to much of the philosophy of the Nibelungen trilogy ; it is in virtue of heroic renunciation that Hans Sachs becomes the central figure of the *Meistersinger*, for dignity and pathos ; and the informing idea of *Lohengrin*, also, is that better than all the sunlit joys of life, dearer than woman's favor and men's homage, stands the law of obedience to some master who is not of this world,—and the Swan Knight leaves his Elsa and his fair kingdom for an empire of shadow. It is not enough to say that the stuff of all tragedy is just this thing—a noble soul's voluntary acceptance of the sharp decrees of higher law. The individual qualities of Wagner's tragic conceptions are in keeping with that Oriental philosophy to which Schopenhauer introduced him. So when, after rejecting both his earlier plans, he came to write *Parsifal*, it is comprehensible enough that the result, however Christian the theme and medieval the material, should betray the influence of his besetting thought.

Now what elements in Wolfram's story lend themselves to such change, not to say distortion? Manifestly the conception of the hero's purity. To bring out this quality and make it a determining factor of the drama, was therefore a temptation Wagner could not resist, although in accomplishing his purpose he must depart essentially from Wolfram. So the "loathly damsel" Kundrie, in Wolfram the Grail Messenger, is endowed with supernatural beauty and with powers of magic, is identified, moreover, with that Herodias who was doomed to walk the earth in fruitless penitence, enticing men to their ruin, until some pure soul should resist her unwillingly-exerted charms. To unify his plot Wagner made Parsifal's power to do this depend on his being touched with pity for Anfortas' pains and with horror at the sin of sensuality which had brought them upon that suffering Grail King. Wagner did no violence to the general spirit of medieval romance, in making celibate chastity the crown of all virtues; but Wolfram was peculiar in differing from his monkish predecessors on just this point, for his Parzival is no ascetic. We cannot, of course, challenge Wagner's right to re-inspire his material and make the flame white or red as he pleased. That he made it white, only proves his dramatic vigor and his vast sweep of view in the study of sources. For he was writing a medieval drama, and surely he produced a more consistent effect thus than he would have done had he strictly followed Wolfram. And, moreover, the conception of abnegation is not solely modern nor Oriental. It is to be found, for example, in the Eddas and in the Celtic myths of Avalon and the Isles beyond the Western Sea. Possibly it has been suggested to all races, at all times, by the sight of death in the young and strong. Wagner's semi-identification of Parsifal with Christ is a proceeding less easily defensible from a dramatic point of view; but in general one may say that this poem is one more evidence, if any were needed after the *Nibelungen* and *Tristan*, of the intellectual supremacy of Richard Wagner. His successive conquests of whole territories of obscure myth and legend are as remarkable as those of the brothers Grimm themselves. The way in which he gathered his substance and harmonized it in *Parsifal* is a grand illustration of the magnetic quality of a soul-possessing idea, which draws all things to itself.

I have been led to accept Nutt's list as the main authority for the order of most of the above cited versions from a belief in the soundness of his two statements, viz: first, an à priori principle that the tendency in bodies of medieval literature is to develop from the racial-heathen towards the Christian-legendary form and not vice versa; and secondly, that the poetical motive of a search or quest of the grail symbols is of older origin than the accounts which various versions give of the Christian origin of those symbols. Furthermore, Mr. Nutt has shown that there existed in Celtic literature abundant suggestion for a grail-myth independent of any Christian source. But it would not be fair to omit to say that the views of Birch-Hirschfeld, which are the reverse of all this, are more simply and clearly sustained than those of Nutt, who seems to labor under his great burden of minute information. I cannot profess to be convinced that Borron's poem may not have been, after all, as Birch-Hirschfeld maintains, written before Chrestien's. The difficulties encountered in this investigation impress me with a sense of how little the best inductive criticism can achieve when once a few bare facts about dates and sources and persons are lost. Birch-Hirschfeld, putting Borron first, and showing how, after monkish fashion, he wove a tale based on holy scripture and apocryphal books, makes Chrestien follow him, while the

mabinogi is an imitation of the *Conte du Graal*. Everyone
must admit, however, that the story of Young Perceval and
many other incidents are of ancient Celtic and non-Christian
origin.

But the power of the Christian conception, and also the trend
of time, making constantly towards Christ, are seen in the subsequent history of the legend.   The poem of Wolfram, later
and more perfect than the French originals, is no less than
the story of Mansoul lifted out of grossness, despite dark doubt,
by aspiration after God as He is manifested in the mystery of
the Grail. *Parzival* is a noble forerunner of *Faust;* it makes
the same bitter cry for the same sad woes; it leads through
unbelief to triumphant faith; it teaches, finally, that spiritual
attainment cannot be, until the soul forgets herself in humble
sympathy for the sorrows of others.   And this poem of the
Middle Ages, thus worthy to stand side by side with that
other great product of the spiritual German nation, contains
no moral beauties, the germs of which cannot be found in those
earlier, less serious, less consciously religious Welsh, French,
and English works.

The Grail as typifying the sacrament of the supper, and that
again as symbolizing the continued presence of Christ in the
world, to help and save—this was the final cause, the unac-
knowledged reason, the unknown beginning, of the whole
cycle.) It is as if a divine hand had been holding the hands
of all the writers of these books; and there can be few plainer
triumphs of the Christian ideal than this, of having converted
and drawn unto itself an obscure pagan myth, a stupid and
unhistorical monkish fiction, many vain and worldly "adventures," until they appear at last fused into one as Wolfram's
Parzival, as Tennyson's *Holy Grail*, as Wagner's *Parsifal*.
In whatever shape, of mere frivolous romance, or of mythological tradition, or of garrulous monkish invention, the legend
may have originated, its destiny was, to become increasingly
moral, to embody a most spiritual religious doctrine; and
whether or no its kernel is a survival of Druidical ceremonies

and superstitions, its character developed more and more in the direction of Christian symbolism. Words alone, beautiful as Wagner's are, did not seem to this greatest of modern Germans capable of holding the intense fervor of his theme; and the legend has found its latest expression in the latest and most wonderful art of man's invention, the music-drama, and in the supreme work of that art's first master. Wagner wrote his poem in fuller accord with the medieval conception than Tennyson, as he was obliged to do in order to preserve the sense of objective reality necessary in an acted drama, the medieval story being in all points capable of scenic representation. Tennyson, as we know, has transcendentalized it, employing the later, Christian-legendary account, and not the mythological one.

> "The cup, the cup itself, from which our Lord
> Drank at the last sad supper with his own.
> This, from the blessed land of Aromat—
> After the day of darkness, when the dead
> Went wandering o'er Moriah—the good saint,
> Arimathaean Joseph, journeying brought
> To Glastonbury, where the winter thorn
> Blossoms at Christmas, mindful of our Lord.
> And there awhile it bode: and if a man
> Could touch or see it, he was heal'd at once,
> By faith, of all his ills."

What thing the Grail was, Percivale's sister, the ecstatic nun, essays to tell:

> "Sweet brother, I have seen the Holy Grail:
> For, waked at dead of night, I heard a sound
> As of a silver horn from o'er the hills
> Blown, and I thought, 'It is not Arthur's use
> To hunt by moonlight;' and the slender sound
> As from a distance beyond distance grew
> Coming upon me—O never harp nor horn,
> Nor aught we blow with breath, or touch with hand,
> Was like that music as it came; and then
> Stream'd through my cell a cold and silver beam,
> And down the long beam stole the Holy Grail,

> Rose-red with beatings in it, as if alive,
> Till all the white walls of my cell were dyed
> With rosy colors leaping on the wall;
> And then the music faded, and the Grail
> Pass'd, and the beam decay'd, and from the walls
> The rosy quiverings died into the night."

No other version equals Tennyson's description of the origin of the quest:

> " 'Then of a summer night it came to pass.
> While the great banquet lay along the hall,
> That Galahad would sit down in Merlin's chair.
> And all at once, as there we sat, we heard
> A cracking and a riving of the roofs,
> And rending, and a blast, and overhead
> Thunder, and in the thunder was a cry.
> And in the blast there smote along the hall
> A beam of light seven times more clear than day:
> And down the long beam stole the Holy Grail
> All over covered with a luminous cloud,
> And none might see who bore it, and it past.
> But every knight beheld his fellow's face
> As in a glory, and all the knights arose,
> And staring each at other like dumb men
> Stood, till I found a voice and swore a vow.
>   I swore a vow before them all, that I,
> Because I had not seen the Grail, would ride
> A twelvemonth and a day in quest of it,
> Until I found and saw it, as the nun
> My sister saw it; and Galahad swore the vow,
> And good Sir Bors, our Lancelot's cousin, swore,
> And Lancelot swore, and many among the knights,
> And Gawain swore, and louder than the rest.' "

And so on through those familiar lines describing how Galahad attained to perfect vision and Percivale to such a sight that henceforth he

> "cared but to pass into the silent life,"

and Lancelot, for his sin, was granted only a terrific glimpse.

Tennyson's melodious creation is known to all, and haunts the memory like one of Doré's dream-cities, with clustering and forehead-meeting towers. Wagner's is compounded of poetry and the indescribable and not-to-be-discussed diviner art of music. But Wolfram's *Parzival*, the only great poem by a single known author between the Latin classics and Dante, might be described briefly and made to show what pre-Dantean medieval art was. I have attempted to translate a few of Wolfram's rapid and somewhat uncouth verses. The original metre and rhyming system have been for the most part preserved, my aim being as much literalness as is consistent with clearness and grace. Indeed, in all but a few passages of overweening tenderness and beauty, Wolfram himself seems to aspire rather to force than to elegance, as became a warrior, who disclaimed all purpose of trying to win favor by words,

> When Love's the stake and Knighthood plays.

The poem is in sixteen books of about 1,550 lines each. The versification is irregular, iambic tetrameter being, however, by far the most frequent form of the verses, which rhyme in successive pairs, but not necessarily in couplets: that is to say, two rhyming lines belong frequently to different sentences, so that the assonance is sometimes purely artificial and void of all pleasing effect.

The first two books, which are considered to have been written last, are filled, after a few introductory lines, with the adventures of Parzival's father Gahmuret,—incidents which have no connection with the Grail or any of the leading threads of narrative which follow. In the words of prelude, however, Wolfram does announce one of the moral motives of his work. They begin as follows:

> When doubt a human conscience gnaws,
> Peace from that breast her light withdraws.
> Beauty and ugliness we find
> Even in the bravest heart combined,
> If taint be in him, great or slight,
> As in the magpie black and white.
> Yet ofttimes may he saved be,

For both share in his destiny—
High heaven and the abyss of hell.
But when the man is infidel
Of midnight blackness is his soul,
His course is towards yon pitchy hole;
While he of steady mind pursues
The shining road the righteous choose.

True to his Germanic blood, Wolfram introduces his hearers
at once into an atmosphere of moral inquiry, and the subject of
his poem is not mere courtly adventure, tinged with religious
mysticism, as is the case with the French, Welsh, and English
versions, but besides this and underlying it, the eternal warfare
of doubt against the soul's activity.   The rest of his introduction is broadly executed, being a rambling discourse on fidelity,
love, and woman, to our ears a strange medley of grave and
humorous.   And then he plunges into the recital of Gahmuret's
adventures.   The fact that they have no essential connection
with the rest of the poem shows how fond were medieval audi-
ences of mere narration for its own sake.   Wolfram briefly
praises his unborn hero Parzival, a man of unalloyed courage,
to whom fear and deceit were unknown, and then tells how his
father Gahmuret, the younger son of Gandein, king of Anjou,
enters the service of the Kalif of Bagdad, winning the love of
the heathen queen Belakane, whom he forsakes because she will
not become a Christian.   He subsequently marries a lady named
Herzeloide.   He is slain in battle, and Herzeloide, hearing the
news, buries herself in the wilderness of Soltane with her son,
whom she resolves to protect from his father's fate by keeping
him in ignorance of chivalry and warfare.

Then begins the recital proper, the first episode, which I
have translated, being the idyllic story of Parzival's youth,
told much more fully and picturesquely by Wolfram than by
any of the other romancers.   For the purposes of scientific investigation it would be better to consider this incident in one
of the older accounts, such as the mabinogi, but if we are con-
cerned to feel the pulse-beat of the highest poetic fervor attained

by any of the old writers of the cycle, we must seek it here. Indeed, as Wolfram is acknowledged to be the most profound and at times the sweetest of the old German singers, and as none of his other work equals this episode in tenderness and spring-like freshness, it has always appealed to me as the most beautiful sustained passage in medieval literature previous to Dante.

> Another may with worthier thought
> Of women speak—I hate him not;
> I court their favor everywhere;
> Only to one no meed I bear
> Of service humble and true;
> Towards her my wrath is ever new
> Since first she harmed me with a lie.
> Wolfram von Eschenbach am I—
> Can bear a part in all your songs;
> And fast, as with a pair of tongs,
> For her I hold resentment hot
> Who such affliction on me brought.
> How can I help but hate her, who
> Gave me such harsh misdeeds to rue?
> Why other ladies hate me then,
> Alack, that is beyond my ken!
>
> If their dislike does me no good,
> Still 'tis a proof of womanhood,
> And since my words were none too fine,
> To bear the blame be also mine!
> This shall not soon again befall,
> But if it does I warn you all,
> Good ladies, storm not as before
> My house about my ears. Of war
> I understand the tactics quite;
> Your foibles and your faults I might
> Too well disclose. But for a pure
> And modest woman I'd endure
> All bitter strife; to ease her woe
> My heart would fain all joys forgo.
>
> On broken crutches halts his fame
> Who, angered by his scornful dame,
> Dares to speak ill of womankind.
> And first, that none offense may find,
> With poet's arts I'll not ensnare
> Her who may grant me audience fair.

A knight-at-arms am I by birth;
In me sleep warlike strength and worth;
She who might love me for my song
Would show a judgment sadly wrong.
For if I seek a lady's grace
And may not go before her face
With honors won by shield and sword,
I will not woe her, by my word!
No other game can have my praise
When Love's the stake and Knighthood plays.
And seeméd it not flattery
Of ladies, I should let you see
Straight to the end of my narration
And much that's new in the creation.
If anyone enjoys the tale
Let him take notice, without fail,
This is no book. Letters I know not.
To them for leaven I go not,
As others use; and these adventures
Shall come to end without such censures.
Rather than have them thought a book
I'd naked sit, without a smock,—
That is, in a bath-tub 't would be,
With a bathing-towel to cover me.

I find the usage much to blame
Which makes no difference in the name
Of women false and women true.
Clear-voiced are all, but not a few
Quickly to evil courses run,
While others every folly shun.
So goes the world, but still 'tis shame
The bad ones share that honored name.
Loyal and fair is womanhood,
When once the name is understood.

Many there are who cannot see
Anything good in poverty.
But he who bears its trials well
May save his faithful soul from hell!
These trials once a woman bore
And gained thereby of grace a store.
Not many in their youth resign
Riches in life for wealth divine.
I know not one in all the earth,
Whate'er the sex or age or birth,
For mortals all in this agree.

But Herzeloide the rich ladie
From her three lands afar did go—
She bore such heavy weight of woe.
In her was no unfaithfulness,
As every witness did confess.
All dark to her was now the sun;
The world's delights she fain would shun.
Alike to her were night and day,
For sorrow followed her alway.
Now went the mourning lady good
Forth from her realm into a wood
In Soltane the wilderness;
Not for flowers, as you might guess;
Her heart with sorrow was so full
She had no mind sweet flowers to pull,
Red though they were and bright, or pale.
She brought with her to that safe vale
Great Gahmuret's her lord's young child.
Her servants, with them there exiled,
Tilled the scant glebe with hoe and plough.
To run with them she'd oft allow
Her son. And e'er his mind awoke
She summoned all this vassal folk,
And on them singly, woman and man,
She laid this strange and solemn ban:
Never of knights to utter word,
"For if of them my darling heard,
And knightly life and knightly fare,
'Twould be a grief to me and care.
Now guard your speech and hark to me,
And tell him naught of chivalrie."
With troubled mien they all withdrew
And so concealed the young boy grew
Soltane's greenwood far within.
No royal sports he might begin
Save one—to draw the bow
And bring the birds above him low
With arrows cut by his own hand,
All in that forest land.
But when one day a singing bird
He shot, and now no longer heard
Its thrilling note, he wept aloud,
This boy so innocent yet proud,
And beat his breast and tore his hair
This boy so wild yet wondrous fair.

At the spring in the glade
He every day his toilet made.
Free had he been from sorrow
Till now when he must borrow
Sweet pain from birds.
Into his heart their music pressed
And swelled it with a strange unrest.
Straight to the queen he then did run;
She said: "Who hurt thee, pretty son?"
But nought could he in answer say—
'Tis so with children in our day.

    Long mused the queen what this might be,
Till once beneath a greenwood tree
She saw him gazing and sighing still,
Then knew 'twas a bird's song did fill
Her darling's breast with yearning pain
And haunting mystery.

    Queen Herzeloide's anger burned
Against the birds, she knew not why;
Her serving-folk she on them turned
And bade to quench their hated cry,
And chase and beat and kill
In every brake, on every hill.
Few were the birds that flew away
And saved their lives in that fierce fray;
Yet some escaped to live and sing
Joyous, and make the forest ring.

    Unto the queen then spoke the boy:
"Why do you rob them of their joy?"
Such intercession then he made,
His mother kissed him while she said:
"Why should I break God's law and rob
The birds of innocent delight?"
Then to his mother spoke the boy:
"O mother, what is God?"

    "My son, in solemn truth I say
He is far brighter than the day,
Though once his countenance did change
Into the face of man.
O son of mine, give wisely heed,
And call on Him in time of need,
Whose faithfulness has never failed
Since first the world began.
And one there is, the lord of hell,
Black and unfaithful, as I tell;

Bear thou towards him a courage stout,
And wander not in paths of doubt."
  His mother taught him to discern
Darkness and light; he quick did learn.
The lesson done, away he'd spring
To practice with the dart and sling.
Full many an antlered stag he shot
And home to his lady mother brought;
Through snow or floods, it was the same,
Still harried he the game.
Now hear the tale of wonder:
When he had brought a great stag low,
Burden a mule might stagger under,
He'd shoulder it and homeward go!
  Now it fell out upon a day
He wandered down a long wood-way
And plucked a leaf and whistled shrill,
Near by a road that crossed a hill.
And thence he heard sharp hoof-strokes ring,
And quick his javelin did swing,
Then cried: "Now what is this I hear?
What if the devil now appear,
With anger hot, and grim?
But, certain, I will not flee him!
Such fearful things my mother told—
I ween her heart is none too bold."
  All ready thus for strife he stood,
When lo! there galloped through the wood
Three riders, shining in the light,
From head to foot in armor dight.
The boy all innocently thought
Each one a god, as he was taught.
No longer upright then stood he,
But in the path he bent his knee.
Aloud he called, and clear and brave,
"Save, God, for thou alone canst save!'
The foremost rider spoke in wrath
Because the boy lay in the path:
"This clumsy Welsh boy
Hinders our rapid course."
A name we Bavarians wear
Must the Welsh also bear:
They are clumsier even than we,
But good fighters too, you'll agree.

A graceful man within the round
Of these two lands is rarely found.
    That moment came a knight
In battle-gear dedight,
Galloping hard and grim
Over the mountain's rim.
The rest had ridden on before,
Pursuing two false knights, who bore
A lady from his land.
That touched him near at hand;
The maid he pitied sore,
Who sadly rode before.
After his men he held his course,
Upon a fine Castilian horse.
His shield bore marks of many a lance;
His name—Karnacharnanz,
Le comte Ulterlec.
    Quoth he: "Who dares to block our way?"
And forth he strode to see the youth,
Who thought him now a god in sooth,
For that he was a shining-one:
His dewy armor caught the sun,
And with small golden bells were hung
The stirrup-straps, that blithely swung
Before his greavéd thighs
And from his feet likewise.
Bells on his right arm tinkled soft
Did he but raise his hand aloft.
Bright gleamed that arm from many a stroke,
Warded since first to fame he woke.
Thus rode the princely knight,
In wondrous armor dight.
    That flower of manly grace and joy,
Karnacharnanz, now asked the boy:
"My lad, hast seen pass by this way
Two knights that grossly disobey
The rules of all knight-errantry?
For with a helpless maid they flee,
Whom all unwilling they have stolen,
To honor lost, with mischief swollen."
The boy still thought, despite his speech,
That this was God, for so did teach
His mother Herzeloide, the queen—
To know Him by his dazzling sheen.
He cried in all humility:

"Help, God, for all help comes from thee!'
And fell in louder suppliance yet
Le fils du roi Gahmuret.
    "I am not God," the prince replied,
"Though in his law I would abide.
Four knights we are, couldst thou but see
What things before thine eyes be."
    At this the boy his words did stay:
"Thou namest knights, but what are they?
And if thou hast not power divine
Tell me, who gives, then, knighthood's sign?"
"King Arthur, lad, it is,
And goest thou to him, I wis
That if he gives thee knighthood's name
Thou'lt have in that no cause for shame.
Thou hast indeed a knightly mien."
The chevalier had quickly seen
How God's good favor on him lay.
The legend telleth what I say,
And further doth confirm the boast
That he in beauty was the first
Of men since Adam's time: this praise.
Was his from womankind always.
    Then asked he in his innocence,
Whereon they laughed at his expense:
"Aye, good sir knight, what mayst thou be,
That hast these many rings I see
Upon thy body closely bound
And reaching downward to the ground?"
With that he touched the rings of steel
Which clothed the knight from head to heel,
And viewed his harness curiously.
"My mother's maids," commented he,
"Wear rings, but have them strung on cords,
And not so many as my lord's."
    Again he asked, so bold his heart:
"And what's the use of every part?
What good do all these iron things?
I cannot break these little rings."
    The prince then showed his battle-blade:
"Now look ye, with this good sword's aid,
I can defend my life from danger
If overfallen by a stranger,
And for his thrust and for his blow
I wrap myself in harness so."

Quick spoke the boy his hidden thought:
"'Tis well the forest stags bear not
Such coats of mail, for then my spear
Would never slay so many deer."
   By this the other knights were vexed
Their lord should talk with a fool perplexed.
The prince ended: "God guard thee well,
And would that I had thy beauty's spell!
And hadst thou wit, then were thy dower
The richest one in heaven's power.
May God's grace ever with thee stay."
Whereat they all four rode away,
Until they came to a field
In the dark forest concealed.
There found the prince some peasant-folk
Of Herzeloide with plow and yoke.
Their lot had never been so hard,
Driving the oxen yard by yard,
For they must toil to reap the fruit
Which first was seed and then was root.
   The prince bade them good day,
And asked if there had passed that way
A maiden in distressful plight.
They could not help but answer right,
And this is what the peasants said:
"Two horsemen and a maid
We saw pass by this morning,
The lady, full of scorning,
Rode near a knight who spurred her horse
With iron heel and language coarse."
   That was Meliakanz;
After him rode Karnacharnanz.
By force he wrested the maid from him;
She trembled with joy in every limb.
Her name, Imaine
Of Bellefontaine.
   The peasant folk were sore afraid
Because this quest the heroes made;
They cried: "What evil day for us!
For has young master seen them thus
In iron clad from top to toe,
The fault is ours, ours too the woe!
And the queen's anger sure will fall
With perfect justice on us all,

Because the boy, while she was sleeping,
Came out this morning in our keeping."
    The boy, untroubled by such fear,
Was shooting wild stags far and near;
Home to his mother he ran at length
And told his story; and all strength
Fled from her limbs, and down she sank,
And the world to her senses was a blank.
    When now the queen
Opened her eyelids' screen,
Though great had been her dread
She asked: "Son, tell me who has fed
Thy fancy with these stories
Of knighthood's empty glories?"
"Mother, I saw four men so bright
That God himself gives not more light;
Of courtly life they spoke to me
And told how Arthur's chivalry
Doth teach all knighthood's office
To every willing novice."
    Again the queen's heart 'gan to beat.
His wayward purpose to defeat
She thought her of a plan
To keep at home the little man.
    The noble boy, in simplest course,
Begged his mother for a horse.
Her secret woe broke out anew;
She said: "Albeit I shall rue
This gift, I can deny him nought.
Yet there are men," she sudden thought,
"Whose laughter is right hard to bear,
And if fool's dress my son should wear
On his beautiful shining limbs,
Their scorn will scatter all these whims,
And he'll return without delay."
This trick she used, alack the day!
A piece of coarse sack-cloth she chose
And cut thereout doublet and hose,
From his neck to his white knees,
And all from one great piece,
With a cap to cover head and ears,
For such was a fool's dress in those years.
Then instead of stockings she bound
Two calfskin strips his legs around.

None would have said he was the same,
And all who saw him wept for shame.
    The queen, with pity, bade him stay
Until the dawn of a new day;
"Thou must not leave me yet," beseeching,
"Till I have given thee all my teaching:
On unknown roads thou must not try
To ford a stream if it be high;
But if it's shallow and clear
Pass over without fear.
Be careful everyone to greet
Whom on thy travels thou mayst meet,
And if any greybearded man
Will teach thee manners, as such men can,
Be sure to follow him, word and deed;
Despise him not, as I thee reed.
One special counsel, son, is mine:
Wherever thou, for favor's sign,
Canst win a good woman's ring or smile,
Take them, thy sorrows to beguile.
Canst kiss her too, by any art,
And hold her beauty to thy heart,
'Twill bring thee luck and lofty mood,
If she chaste is, and good.
    "Lachelein, the proud and bold,
Won from thy princes of old—
I'd have thee know, O son of mine—
Two lands that should be fiefs of thine,
Waleis and Norgals.
One of thy princes, Turkentals,
Received his death from this foe's hands;
And on thy people he threw bands."
    "Mother, for that I'll vengeance wreak;
My javelin his heart shall seek."
    Next morning at first break of day
The proud young warrior rode away.
The thought of Arthur filled his mind.
Herzeloide kissed him and ran behind.
The world's worst woe did then befall.
When no more she saw young Parzival
(He rode away. Whom bettered be?)
The queen from every falseness free
Fell to the earth, where anguish soon
Gave her Death's bitter boon.
Her loyal death

Saves her from hell's hot breath.
'Twas well she had known motherhood!
Thus sailed this root of every good,
Whose flower was humility,
Across that rich-rewarding sea.
Alas for us, that of her race
Till the twelfth age she left no trace!
Hence see we so much falsehood thrive.
Yet every loyal woman alive
For this boy's life and peace should pray,
As he leaves his mother and rides away.

In the remainder of the third book and in the fourth,
Parzival meets with many adventures and incurs a great
deal of trouble in following his mother's singular advice, and
reaches Arthur's court only to be laughed at for his out-
landish garb. But he comes away determined to win a place
for himself at the Round Table. The counsels of his mother
are supplemented by the advice of a wise man, Gurnemanz,
whom he encounters, to the effect that he must never ask
questions, no matter what may excite his curiosity. His days
are henceforth spent in riding on in the hope of finding fit
occasions for exercising his bravery and gallantry. In Book V
he encounters, one evening, a sad-faced, richly-dressed Fisher
beside a lake, who directs him to his castle, where he will find
refreshment. On riding thither Parzival finds grass in the
court-yard, a sign that no jousting takes place there. He is
well received and bidden presently to appear before the Fisher-
King, who turns out to be the old man whom he met fishing.
Him he finds wrapped in furs upon a couch beside the middle
one of three great marble fireplaces in the hall. This spacious
apartment is illuminated by a hundred chandeliers and contains a hundred other couches, on each of which recline four
knights. Aromatic wood blazes on the hearths. Parzival
now is bidden to take his place beside the king. Presently a
young attendant bears through the hall a long lance dripping
blood. At this sight all the spectators break forth into cries
of lamentation. A stately and magnificently-attired band of

noble ladies now enter, bearing candles and the appurtenances of a banquet. At last appears the queen-maiden Repanse de Schoie herself, who for her purity is permitted to carry the Grail. This she sets before the king, and retires to the midst of her four and twenty virgins. Then a hundred tables are brought in and set, on each of which other attendants place a bowl of water and a towel for hand-washing. Each table is waited upon by four pages, with every mark of religious awe. Four wagons roll through the hall with drinking vessels, which are distributed to all the tables. A hundred pages take from before the Grail white napkins containing bread, which they distribute, and from the Grail indeed come food and drink to all desiring. Parzival, mindful of Gurnemanz' counsel, forbears to ask the meaning of these marvels, and remains silent even when the king, presenting him with a costly sword, mentions that he is suffering from a grievous wound.

When the repast is concluded, the food and utensils disappear in the same order in which they came. There is evident disappointment at something Parzival has done or failed to do, but he is led away to sleep in a grand chamber, where dreams torment him in the night, and where he awakes in solitude next day, to find his armor at his bedside and preparations made for his immediate departure. In vain he calls. The castle is empty and silent, and he rides forth at last in troubled wonder. A page instantly raises the drawbridge behind him and reproaches him for not having questioned his host. He presently encounters a lady, who tells him he has been on Montsalvat, where no man arrives except unknowingly. When she learns of his omission to inquire the meaning of what he saw, she blames him bitterly for the fatal mistake, and he rides sadly away. The king was Anfortas, keeper of the Grail. All this, and Parzival's failure to inquire the cause of his wound, are announced to Arthur and the knights, on Parzival's return among them, by Kundrie [1] the sorceress, the

---

[1] There is in this Kundrie, "the loathly damsel," the bearer of the Grail's decrees, as treated variously in the different romances, a hint of the Germanic Walküre, and more than a hint of Herodias.

dreadful messenger of the Grail. She curses Parziva'l, who in despair, and distrusting even God himself, rides forth once more, dedicating his life to the quest of the sacred symbol. Those knights whom he overcomes with his spear he sends on parole to seek the Grail for him.

Omitting the long series of adventures by Gawan and others, and by Parzival himself, which intervene, we find him in the ninth book overcoming a knight of the Grail who has offered him battle because he came too near Montsalvat. Parzival takes the knight's horse, which wears the sign of the Grail, a dove. On Good Friday Parzival turns in at the hut of a hermit, who reproves him for his irreligion, and to whom Parzival confesses that for several years he has not set foot in a house of God because of the hatred he bears in his heart toward Him. The hermit instructs him in heavenly matters and especially in the history of the Grail, whose divine origin he sets forth. It is a rich and wondrous stone, called *lapis exillis*, endowed with miraculous power of sustaining life. It has the virtue of gathering about it those whom it elects, and by them it is watched. Anfortas, king of these knights and chief guardian of the Grail, sinned in seeking earthly love, and was sore wounded. Only one thing could restore him: spontaneous inquiry into his condition by some one who should arrive unwittingly at the Grail Castle. When the hermit learns that his guest has had this opportunity and failed to accept it, he blames him severely and tells him further of the mystic art of the stone: how every Good Friday a dove comes down from heaven and places the sacramental wafer on it, and how it indicates its chosen keepers in a miraculous writing which appears upon its side.

Fourteen days pass thus in high converse between Parzival and the hermit, until the latter absolves the young knight, now filled with the one longing—to find his name written on the divine stone. And in the fifteenth book, while sitting at Arthur's Round Table, after many days of weary search, he is surprised by Kundrie the messenger, with the news that he has been chosen King of the Grail, and that his son Loherangrin shall succeed him in that office. He hastens to the Castle, casts himself before the Grail, and asks Anfortas the cause of his pain. Instantly the aged sufferer is healed and becomes beautiful as sunlight. The former ceremony is repeated with great splendor.

The poet then relates how Loherangrin was sent as husband to the young duchess of Brabant, how a swan drew him to Antwerp in a boat, how the duchess disobeyed his request, which was the Grail's command, not to seek to know his origin, and how in sorrow he withdrew.[1]

From a poem of 24,810 verses it has been impossible to give more than the absolutely essential features referring to the Grail. There are long passages which would repay reading even yet, either in the original or in Simrock's very literal translation into modern German. When we compare the moral elements of Wolfram's story with those of the Faust legend as Goethe found them, the question arises : What might not a modern German poet make of this great epic of faith? Although originality of incident may be denied Wolfram, yet it seems to me that the spirit of his story, and particularly of the Young Parzival episode, is both personal and national. The recognition of a close relation between theology and conduct is one thing which distinguishes Wolfram's *Parzival* from all earlier versions of the legend.

_____

APPENDIX A.—Translation of extract from Wolfram given on pages 32–34 :

From him now Parzival learns the hidden story of the Grail. If anyone had asked me about it before, and been angry at me for not telling it to him, his grumbling would have been in vain. Kiot bade me keep it secret, because the "Aventure" commanded him to guard it still undivulged ; no one was to learn it until in the course of the narration the time came to speak of it. Kiot, the well-known master, found in Toledo,

_____

[1] This request and its consequence, like Parzival's refraining to ask concerning Anfortas and the troubles caused by his not doing so, point to the ultimate connection between this romance material and the fairy literature not only of Europe, but of Asia.

lying thrown away, and in heathen writing, the story which treats of the Grail. He must first have been acquainted with the characters A, B, C, without necromancy. The grace of baptism stood him there in good stead, or the story would be still untold. No heathen art could e'er avail us to disclose what is revealed of the Grail's character and power. A heathen, Flegetanis, was held in esteem for his rare arts. A seer, he descended from Solomon, arriving from Israelitish blood ages ago, before baptism was our shield against the torment of hell. He wrote about the Grail's history. He was a heathen on his father's side, this Flegetanis, who still prayed to a calf as if it were his God. How dare the devil work such contempt on such wise peoples? Will the hand of the All-highest, to whom all wonders are manifest, not deign to keep them from it? Flegetanis the heathen could announce to us well the outgoing course of all the stars and their future return —how long each has to go till we see it at its goal. Human fate and being are to be read in the march of the stars. Flegetanis, the heathen, when he turned his gaze toward heaven, discovered mysterious lore. He spake thereof with hesitating tongue: There is a thing called the Grail. In the stars found he its name written as it is called. "A company which flew again to heaven, whether drawn home by grace or disfavor, left it on the earth. Then baptised fruit [Christians] tended it with humility and pure discipline. Those men are always worthy who are required for the Grail's service." Thus Flegetanis wrote of it. Kiot, the master wise, began to seek in Latin books where there could ever have been people worthy the honor of tending the Grail and nourishing chastity in their hearts. He read the national chronicles in Britain and elsewhere, in France and Ireland, until he found the story in Anjou. There in unfailing truth he read about Mazadan, and found all written correctly about his race; and on the other hand how Titurel and his son Frimutel delivered the Grail to Anfortas, whose sister was called Herzeloide, by whom Gahmuret had a child, of whom these stories tell.

APPENDIX B.—Meaning of the name Fisher King.

I must beg attention here for a speculation of my own, which, being nothing more, should not be allowed to affect the questions still at issue regarding the origin of the legend, especially as Professor Rhŷs and Mr. Nutt, with something more than speculation, have developed an entirely contradictory idea. They connect the episodes of the Fisher King, and this appellation itself, with a number of Irish stories, for which great antiquity is claimed, and which do indeed seem related to the pagan mythology of Scandinavia. But it has occurred to me that the fishing of the king may have been attributed to him because of his name, and that the names Roi Pêcheur and Fisher King are only old translations of the word Herodius, which itself was wrongly written for Herodes. Attention was long ago, in Germany, called to the numerous allusions to St. John the Baptist that occur in the Grail legends. San Marte and Simrock, fifty years ago, pointed out the resemblance between the Grail knights (in Wolfram called Templeisen) and the Templars, who were accused of worshipping a miracle-working head. In the mabinogi the Grail is a salver containing a man's head floating in blood. Wagner's treatment of Kundrie is not far from what seems to have been an idea hovering in the minds of some of the earliest creators of the legend, namely that she was Herodias, or possibly the daughter of Herodias, pursued by a "cruel immortality." Let us suppose that the "great Latin book," or some lost Latin original, contained the word Herodes where we find *roi pêcheur* in the French. A slovenly or officious copyist might easily make it Herodius. Another copyist or a translator, taking this for a name derived from a common noun, might translate it into French. *Herodius* is the name of a bird. It occurs twice that I know of in the Vulgate: in Deuteronomy 14, 16, where the English has "the little owl," and in Psalm 104 (Vulgate 103), 17, where the English has "stork." The exact meaning of *herodius* is unknown, but it would not be strange if this copyist or translator had rendered it by *roi pêcheur*, English kingfisher.

GEORGE McLEAN HARPER.